THE
XRISTOS FACTOR
TIP OF THE SPEAR: CHURCH DISCIPLESHIP REVOLUTION

DR. ROBERT V. MYERS

R
RENOVATE
Publishing Group

The Xristos Factor: Tip of the Spear Church Discipleship Revolution (Study Book)

Xristos Factor
14380 SW 166th Street
Miami, FL 33177
786-256-3054 | xristosfactor.org

ISBN 9987384-2-5
ISBN 978-0-9987384-2-0

Published by Renovate Publishing Group

Ordering Information:

For details, contact the publisher at the address above
Online ordering and purchase: xristosfactor.org

Design/Production by J. Jeffrey Toler

Printed in the United States of America

First Edition: 2017

Scripture references, unless otherwise noted:
The Holy Bible, New International Version. Grand Rapids: Zondervan House, 1984. Print.

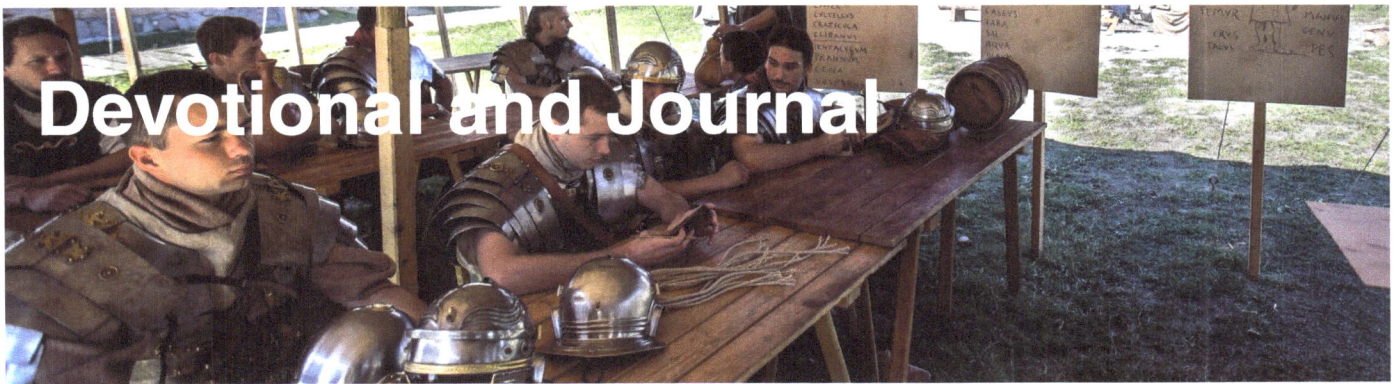

Devotional and Journal

Dear Gentlemen,

Each day begins with the new morning! Do your best to discipline your life to rise early and to go to bed on time. The world belongs to the productive. Time is a precious commodity; use it wisely, for accomplished men are men of the day.

Learn the lesson my dad taught me: have a devotional every day and you will have a better day. Live your life as if you were placed here by God to make a difference; because each of you has a major impact on the people around you. Determine in your heart at the beginning of each day to bring your life into conformity with God's Word.

In Hebrew, the word to meditate means to chew the cud like a cow. The cow has multiple stomachs. The chewing of the cud enables the cow to get all the nutrients out of the grass. In the same way, you are to chew on the Word of God, digest it, and gain all the blessings and nutrients into your being that come from it. Underneath each of the verses for each day, you will see: (read & chew). When you see this, stop and meditate on that part of the Scripture. All Scriptures are RED.

Every day of this 10-week habit-building process involves each of us taking up our cross and following Jesus Christ. The cross is where Christ sacrificed His life for us.

Jesus said in Luke 9:23, "Whoever wants to be My disciple must deny himself, take up his cross daily and follow Me."

(read & chew)

Today, I want you to meditate on Romans 12:1-2:

Therefore, I urge you, brothers and sisters in, view of God's mercy, to offer your bodies as a living sacrifice, holy and pleasing to God—this is your true and proper worship. Do not conform to the pattern of this world, but be transformed by the renewing of your mind. Then you will be able to test and approve what God's will is—His good, pleasing and perfect will.

(read & chew)

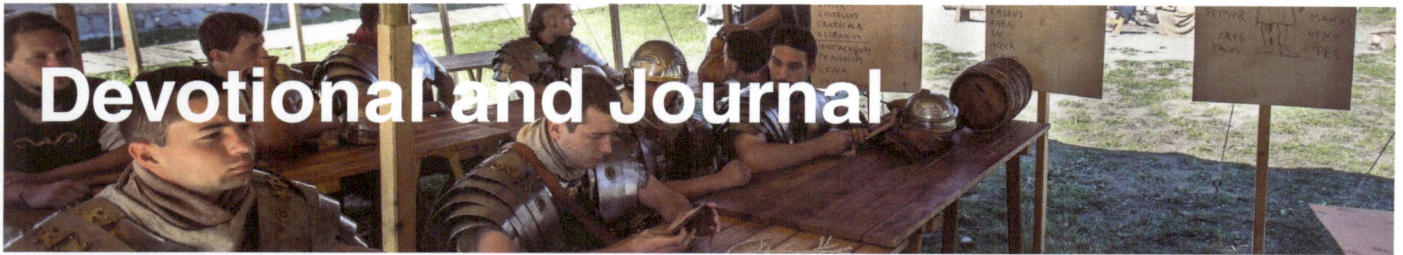

Dear Gentlemen,

As you know, self-centeredness is at the core of all of our sin. This is why Jesus said that if we are to follow Him, we have to take up our cross daily and die to self. This means that in order for us to control "the beast within," we have to make a conscious effort to "bow" self-interest at the foot of the Cross. You will find that this process is not only counter-cultural, but it is also counter-human nature. So don't look to the world to rally behind you as you kill your own self-interest. Only God and Godly men will help you. Surround yourself with a Biblical support system. Remember this: If Jesus Christ had thought that this was a one-time process, He would not have said that we have to die to ourselves daily.

Today, we will look at a new passage that is in a later setting in Luke's Gospel, where Jesus called His men again to radical discipleship. Many of the men who call themselves Christians today have not fully looked at what Christ is asking of a disciple. Today, you are going to meditate on Luke: 14:25-33.

Large crowds were traveling with Jesus, and turning to them He said: "if anyone comes to me and does not hate father and mother, wife and children, brothers and sisters—yes, even their own life—such a person cannot be my disciple."

(read and chew)

Notice, first of all, that the crowds who traveled with Jesus were not necessarily disciples. It would, however, be from those crowds that Jesus would call His disciples to step forward to a supreme commitment. The statement that Jesus makes here is only acceptable if you fully understand that Jesus Christ is God in the flesh; for if a man were to make this challenge as a mere man, he would be considered a megalomaniac. What Jesus is teaching here is that He, Jesus Christ, must be number one, and "in" the God position within our lives. If you cannot make Him number one, you cannot be His disciple.

"And whoever does not carry his cross and follow me cannot be my disciple."

(read and chew)

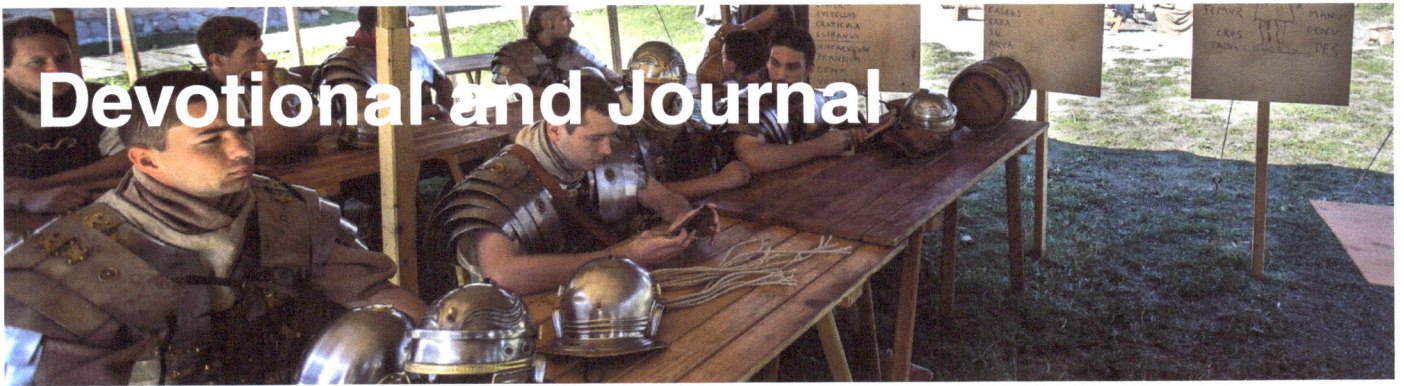

Devotional and Journal

Continued

If you refuse to carry your cross and follow Him, not only can you not be His disciple, but you have moved yourself back to the tenuous position of being a spectator in the crowd.

Today, you must meditate and determine what you are going to do. In Matthew 14, Verses 28-33, Jesus teaches us that you must count the cost and choose what you will do. Being a disciple is not an easy choice. If you choose to continue with us in the mentoring process, being part of the crowd is not an option, and we would ask that you would remove yourself from this process. We will still love you, but we can only go forward with men who are absolutely committed to being disciples of Jesus Christ.

Prayerfully consider your choice.

> *"When God wants to do an impossible task, He takes an impossible man, and He crushes him."*
>
> Alan Redpath

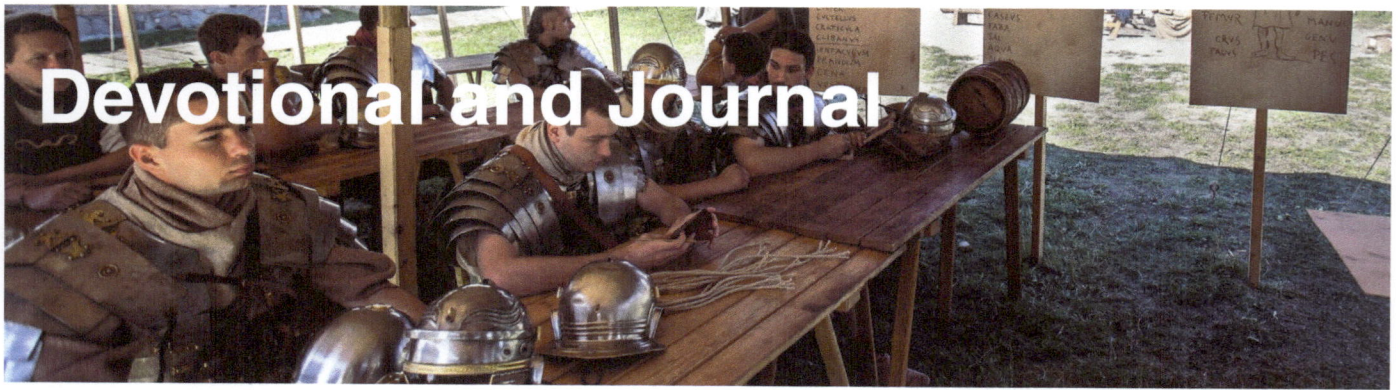

Dear Gentlemen,

It is an honor for a father to have his sons value his advice when they have a life decision to make. I always receive a call or meet with my sons about what they are planning. One thing I've learned is that my heavenly Father loves it when I give Him consideration. It is amazing that we can directly approach the Creator of the world.

Hebrews 10:19 – 25 says:

"Therefore, brothers and sisters, since we have confidence to enter the Most Holy Place by the blood of Jesus, by a new and living way opened for us through the curtain that is His body, and since we have a great priest over the house of God, let us draw near to God with a sincere heart and with the full assurance that faith brings, having our hearts sprinkled to cleanse us from a guilty conscience and having our bodies washed with pure water. Let us hold unswervingly to the hope we profess, for He who promised is faithful. And let us consider how we may spur one another on toward love and good deeds, not giving up meeting together, as some are in the habit of doing, and encouraging one another—and all the more as we see the day approaching."

(read & chew)

We have direct access to God. The thing that keeps us from using the access is our laziness and our lack of discipline to "enter" the presence of God. The sheer desire for personal liberty and independence is misplaced. We must die to ourselves daily and enter with boldness. It is God who desires us to live the victor's life and to not be terrified.

As God committed Joshua to become the new leader of Israel, He said:

"Have I not commanded you? Be strong and courageous. Do not be afraid; do not be discouraged, for the Lord your God will be with you wherever you go." Joshua 1:9

(read & chew)

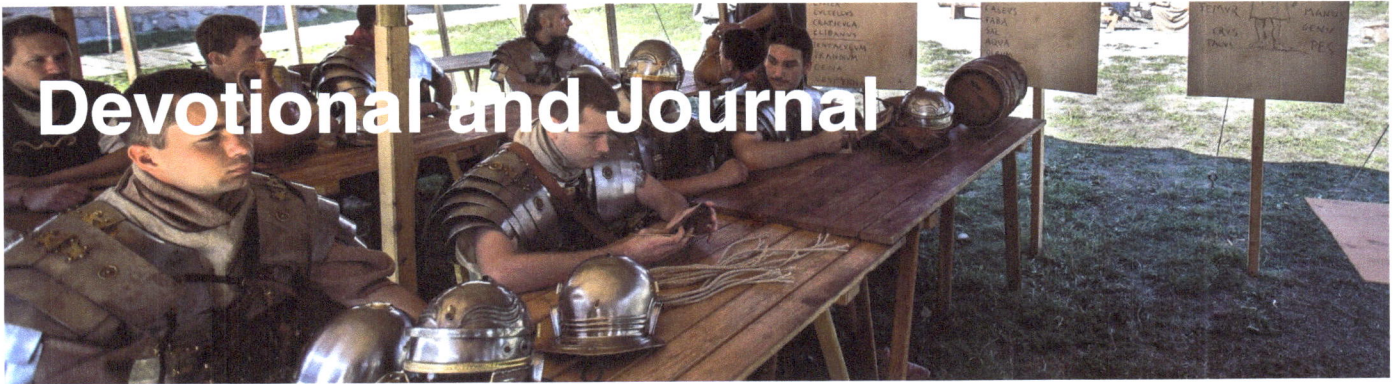

Devotional and Journal

Dear Gentlemen,

Loyalty is one of the most prized character traits in the entire world. One of the greatest measures of a man's character is found by asking a few questions. First: to whom are you loyal? Loyalty is yours to give away, or yours to destroy; so we must choose carefully to whom we are loyal. Under the Lordship of Jesus Christ, God says specifically:

"Do not love the world or anything in this world. If anyone loves the world, love for the Father is not in them." - 1st John 2:15

The relationship God wants with you is exclusive, and to "love Him and Him alone" must be over all—it must be transcendent! All other loyalties are laid at the foot of the Cross. The second question is quantitative: How loyal are you to Him? That is why you must die yourself daily and follow His path. Today, meditate on:

"You have made known to me the path of life; You fill me with joy in Your presence, with eternal pleasures at Your right hand." - Psalm 16:11

(read & chew)

Amidst the ugliness of the Cross, God brings us into His presence and shows us the beauty of His path—there we find true life in Christ!

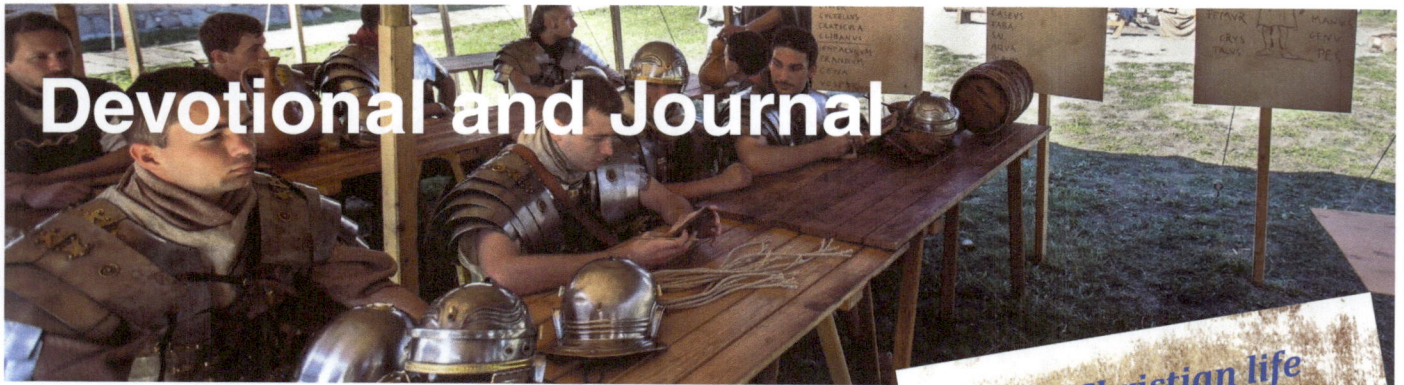

Devotional and Journal

Dear Gentlemen,

"The Christian life doesn't get easier as one gets older."
Alan Redpath

Believe it or not, I vividly remember my life as a young man. From the time puberty hit on, I desperately struggled to control an almost insatiable sexual appetite. I often wondered before God why He had given me something so hard to control that had significant consequences of guilt, and yet felt so good. I found myself vacillating about my opinions of King Solomon; between saying to myself in one moment, "I could never do that," to envying him in my heart the next. Part of me craved sex and lots of it, and the other part of me took a beating with guilt.

I remember hoping that in my older days that "unmanageable urge" would either diminish or pass away. By the way, it never did. Even marriage could not contain it, and I had to learn to daily take this to the foot of the Cross. There are some things in life that have to die once—and then there are some things that have to die every day.

King David was a man after God's own heart. He was by no means sinless, but he was a man who could always find his way back to God.

2nd Samuel, 22:29–37 provides a tremendous insight into how David conquered the lust of his flesh.

"You, Lord, are my lamp; the Lord turns my darkness into light. With Your help I can advance against a troop; with my God I can scale a wall. As for God, His way is perfect: the Lord's Word is flawless; He shields all who take refuge in Him. For who is God besides the Lord? And who is the Rock except our God? It is God who arms me with strength and keeps my way secure. He makes my feet like the feet of a deer; he causes me to stand on the heights. He trains my hands for battle; my arms can bend a bow of bronze. You make your saving help my shield; Your help has made me great. You provide a broad path for my feet so my ankles do not give way."

(read & chew)

I have to walk each day now in the light of Christ Jesus. He is my Rock and my stable place. He is the creator of my soul, and is familiar with my weaknesses. With Him and His Light, I can avoid the darkness of my sin-prone heart. All that I am as a man, I learn from Him. Study the "Manly" traits of King David and determine to be a man after God's own heart. By the way this is a place only reserved for true disciples of God!

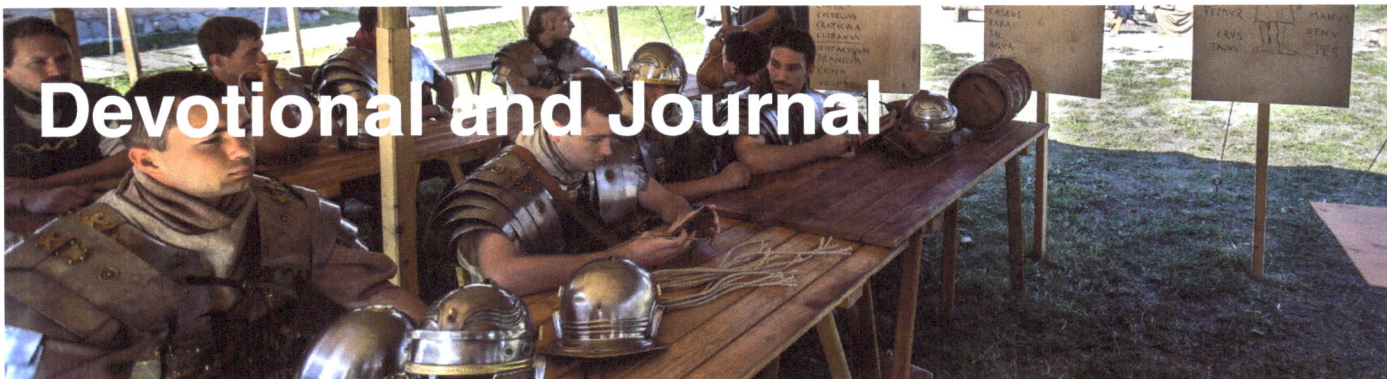

Devotional and Journal

Dear Gentlemen,

In order to live for Christ, there are three areas in a man's life that have to be overcome, that Are "Trinity" of man's fallen nature.

1st. John 2:15 – 17 says:

"Do not love the world or anything in the world. If anyone loves the world, for the father is not in them. For everything in the world – the lust of the flesh, the lust of the eyes, and the pride of life – comes not from the father but from the world. The world and its desires pass away, but whoever does the will of God lives forever."

(read & chew)

Fallen nature number 1 is the lust of the flesh; number 2 is the lust of the eyes; and number 3, is the pride of life. The apostle John gives us a clue as to the source of the evil... The love of the fallen world. Every day I have to ask myself: shall I gratify the desires of my flesh; the fantasies of my eyes and thoughts and will I shake my fist in the face of God and claim my personal rule over my life as in the poem "Invictus?"

Paul says this:

"For if you live according to the flesh, you will die but if by the Spirit you put to death the misdeeds of the body, you will live!" Romans 8:13

(read & chew)

I want you to compare the following two poems. One is entitled Invictus, by Ernest Henley; and the other is entitled When I Survey The Wondrous Cross, by Isaac Watts. Each verse is a diametrically opposed life view.

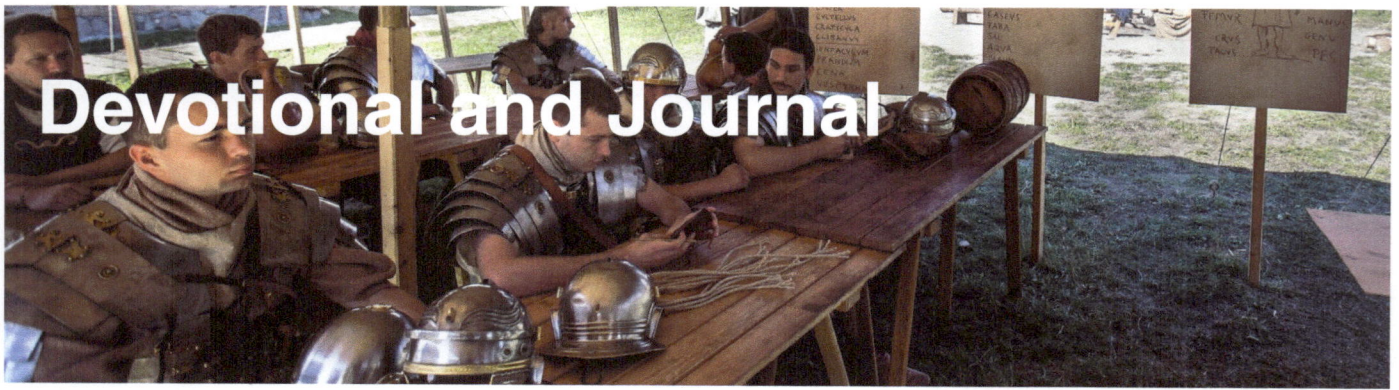

Developmental and Journal

Continued

Invictus, verse 1
Out of the the night that covers me,
Black as the pit from pole to pole,
I thank whatever gods may be,
for my unconquerable soul.

When I Survey The Wondrous Cross, verse 1
When I survey the wondrous Cross,
On which the Prince of Glory died,
My richest gain I count but loss,
And poor contempt on all my pride.

Invictus, verse 2
In the fell clutch of circumstances,
I have not winced nor cried aloud.
Under the bludgeoning of chance,
My head is bloodied, but unbowed.

When I Survey The Wondrous Cross, verse 2
Forbid it, Lord, that I should boast,
Save in the death of Christ, my God!
All the vain things that claim the most,
I sacrifice them to his blood

Invictus, verse 3
beyond this place of wrath and tears,
looms the honor of the shade,
And yet the menace of the years,
Finds and shall find me unafraid.

When I Survey The Wondrous Cross, verse 3
See from His head, His hands, His feet,
Sorrow and love flow mingled down!
Did e'er such love and sorrow meet,
Or thorns compose so rich a Crown?

Invictus, verse 4
It matters not how strait the gate,
How chained with punishments the scroll,
I am the master of my fate,
I am the captain of my soul.

When I Survey The Wondrous Cross, verse 3
Were the whole realm of nature mine,
That were a present far two small,
Love so amazing, so divine,
Demands my soul, my life, my all.

Meditate and think on these things...

"As for me and my house, we will stand on the side of the Cross..."

Will you join us?

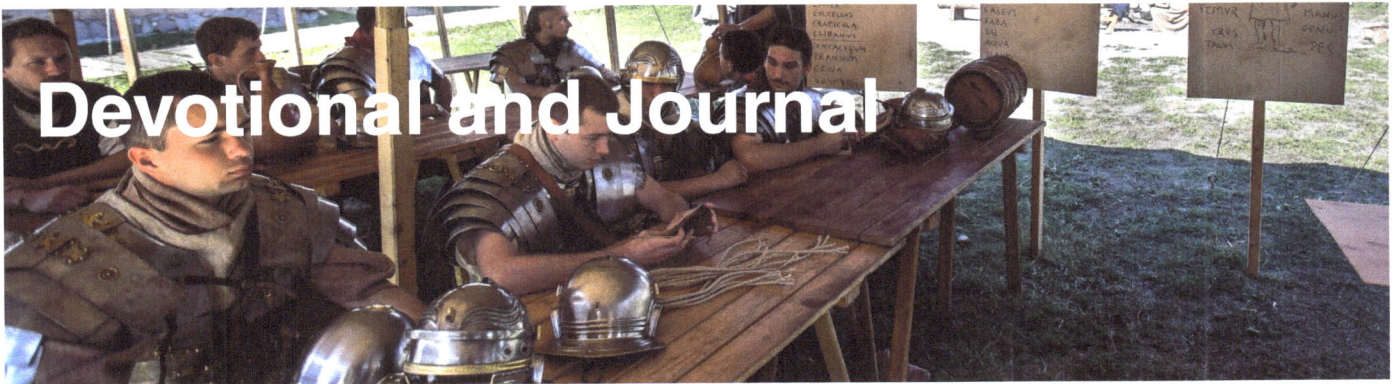

Devotional and Journal

Dear Gentlemen,

We celebrate the Sabbath day of our Lord every day of the week! On the Cross, when Jesus Christ said "tetelesti," He used the term of an accountant, signifying that the account was paid in full. He is interpreted in the King James Version as "It is finished." This signifies that the payment for sin is finished and the account has been settled with our God. The Word teaches us in Hebrews, Chapter 4, verses 9 and 10 that:

"There remains, then, a Sabbath-rest for the people of God; for anyone who enters God's rest also rests from his works, just as God did from His.

(read & chew)

Remember to rest in the finished work of Christ on the Cross. We as believers in Christ have set aside Sunday, which we call the Lord's day, to worship the Lord and to hear the prophetic Word of God preached to our hearts. Bring your mindset into the mindset of Christ on this day, and let your heart offer up personal prayers. Ask yourself the question, "what is not surrendered?" Please surrender at the foot of the Cross and bow the pride of your life before the throne of Christ! Put on the mind of Christ.

Meditate upon Philippians 2:6-11:

"Who, being in the very nature of God, did not consider equality with God something to be used to His own advantage; rather, He made Himself nothing by taking the very nature of a servant, being made in human likeness. And being found in appearance as a man, He humbled Himself by becoming obedient to death—even death on the cross! Therefore God exalted Him to the highest place and gave Him the name that is above every name, that at the name of Jesus every knee should bow, in heaven and on earth and under the earth, and every tongue acknowledge that Jesus Christ is Lord, to the glory of God the Father.

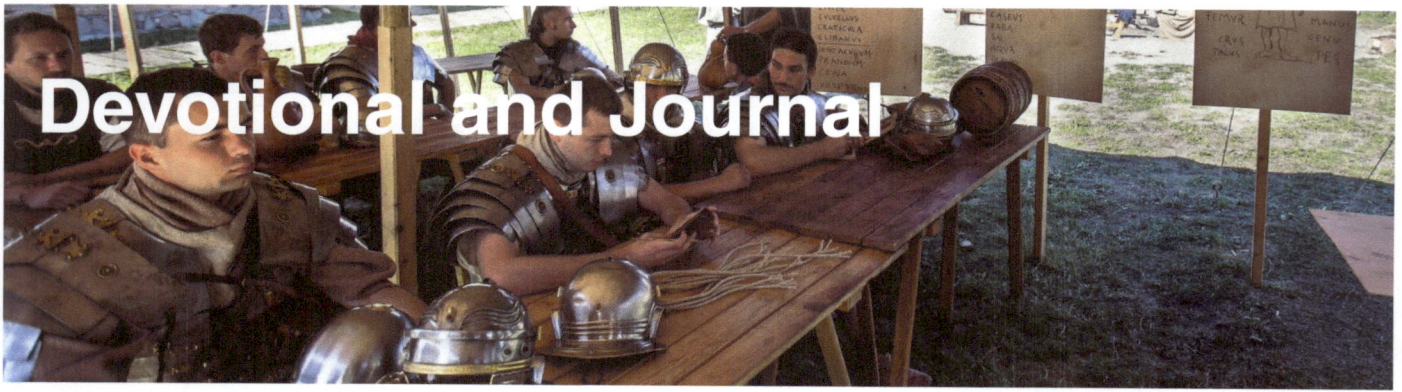

Dear Gentlemen,

Somehow, someway, the Myers are of Jewish descent. It seems that through the tracing of our DNA, along with our name, which is Jewish, one of our ancestors thousands of years ago was of the tribe of Levi. To my brothers in Christ, according to Romans chapter 9, you are adopted Jews who are grafted in to the vine of Israel. An adopted Jew has full rights and privileges before God! In Numbers 15:37 – 41, God gave His men a prescription to help them remember their covenant with Him. This was designed to help them control their lust, by giving their eyes something else to focus on. Today you are receiving a blue-and-white tassel to wear as a bracelet. When you are tempted, I want you to do the following: look at the blue-and-white thread and lay your lust at the foot of Cross.

In that we no longer wear prayer shawls, keep this bracelet on your wrist as a reminder to keep yourself pure. Should you fall into sexual sin, take one of the strands and tie a knot on the end. When you speak to your accountability partner and pray together, you may untie the knot.

Many men fear accountability, in order to survive in this world; however, we must learn to embrace accountability.

"Two are better than one, because they have a good return for their labor: if either of them falls down, one can help the other up. But pity anyone who falls and has no one to help them up. Also, if two lie down together, they will keep warm. But how can one keep warm alone? Though one may be overpowered, two can defend themselves. A cord of three strands is not quickly broken."

Ecclesiastes 4:9 – 12

(read & chew)

Over the course of these 10 weeks, you're going to find a new freedom in Jesus Christ that comes from the power of the twofold cord and the threefold cord. It is your job, and your duty to your brother in Christ with whom you are partnered, to help keep that man from falling. Satan and all of his demons are going to do their very best to keep you from being transparent with your partner. Your partner and your unit can help you defeat sin in your life. As the Scripture says, "do not grow weary in well doing, for at the proper time we will reap a harvest if we do not give up." Galatians 6:9

(read & chew)

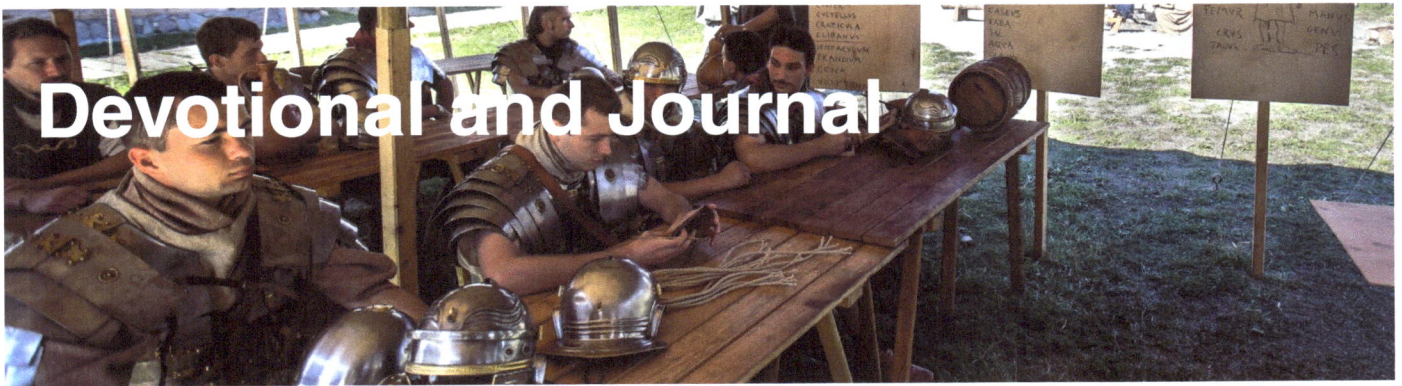

Devotional and Journal

Continued

The following is a poem I learned from my grandfather Myers. Vernon Myers was born in 1896

Don't Quit

When things go wrong,
As they sometimes will;
When the road you're trudging seems all up-hill;
When the funds are low and the debts are high;
And you want to smile, but you have to sigh;
When care is pressing you down a bit:
Rest if you must, but don't you quit.

Life is queer with its twists and turns,
As everyone of us sometimes learns.
And many a fellow turns about,
When he might have won had he stuck it out.
Don't give up though the pace seems slow,
You may succeed with another blow.

Often the goal is nearer than
It seems to a faint and faltering man;
Often the struggler has given up,
When he might have captured the victor's cup;
And he learned too late for the night came down,
How close he was to the Golden Crown.

Success is failure turned inside out,
The silver tint in the clouds of doubt.
It might be near when it seems afar,
So stick to the fight when you're hardest hit.
It's when things seem worst
that you must not quit.

Popular campaign poster: Elections of 1896

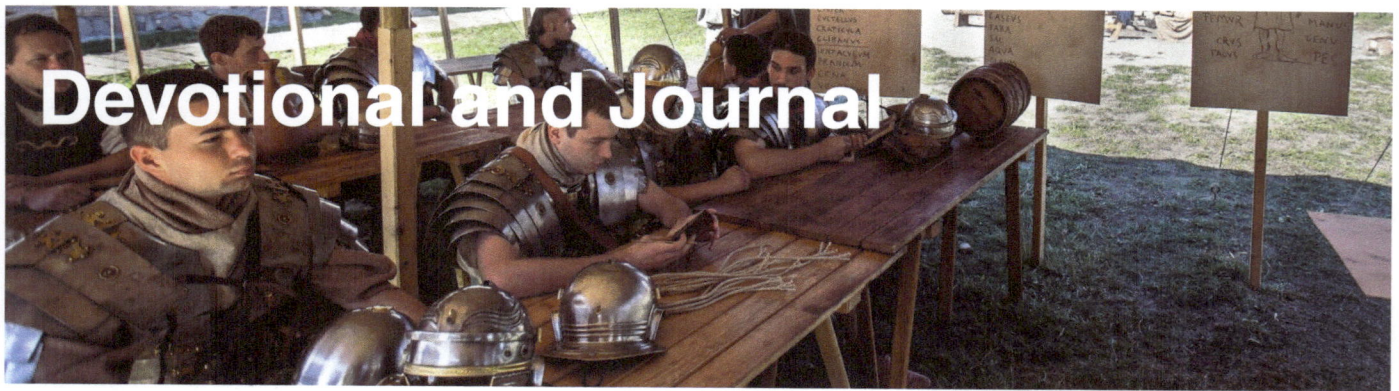

Devotional and Journal

Dear Gentlemen,

Luke 5:1, reveals a subtle key to a healthy walk with God:

"One day as Jesus was standing by the lake of Ginesserat, the people were crowding around Him and listening to The Word of God."

(read & chew)

Just think about this for a moment: when Jesus Christ speaks, what the disciples were hearing was the living Word of God. Now when you read the Word of God, you are hearing the living words of Jesus Christ! In your day-to-day life, take in a daily feeding of the words of Christ! Each week, take on a story of Jesus and place it into your own words... Internalize it; personalize it; and own it.

This Word will live in you and change your character and your mindset. Romans 12:2, teaches us to renew our minds through the Word of God.

"Therefore, I urge you, brothers and sisters, in view of God's mercy, to offer your bodies as a living sacrifice, holy and pleasing to God – this is your true and proper worship. Do not conform to the pattern of this world, but be transformed by the renewing of your mind. Then you will be able to test and approve what God's will is —His good, pleasing and perfect will."

Romans 12:1 & 2

(read & chew)

As you take notes in a journal about what God is teaching you, you'll begin to see tangible changes in your life. As you put more and more words in, you will gain fortitude and strength, which will grow in you a "rock-solid" character.

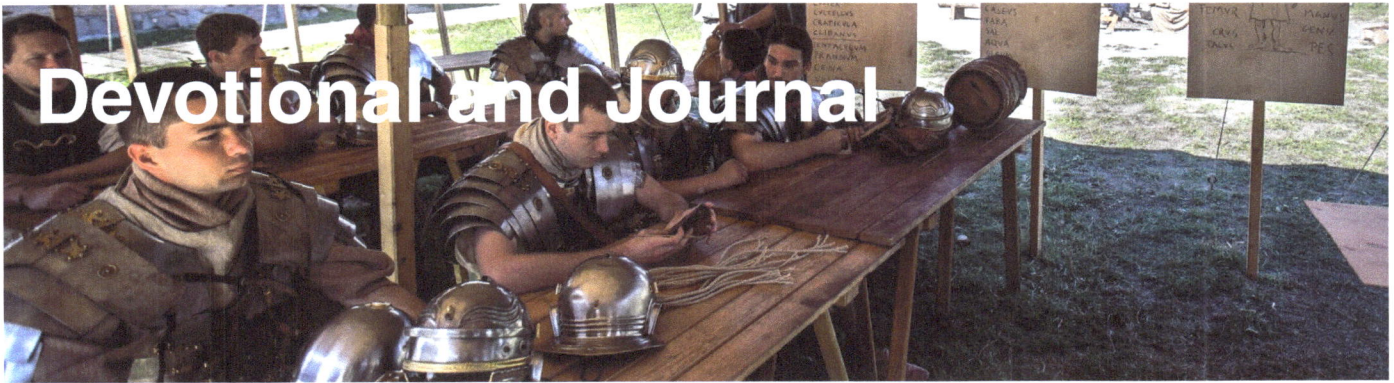

Devotional and Journal

Dear Gentlemen,

Years ago I put someone into my memory by putting it to music.

"Blessed is the man that walketh
not in the counsel of the ungodly,
Nor standeth in the way of the sinner,
Nor sitteth in the seat of the scornful.

Psalm1 (read & chew)

So, as godly men, there are three things we choose not to do. First, we don't go to non-Christians for advice and counseling. The second thing is, we don't live or stand in the lifestyles of sinners and unbelievers.

Gentlemen, if you do not wisely follow these principles, you will find yourself incrementally sliding into a compromised lifestyle.

The third point that we glean from the passage is this: never... I say never (and I say it again for emphasis), never join the whiners or the scornful. At that point, you have become an enemy of the Faith. And to men who scorn the faith of others, I say to them in the words of Jesus: "how dare you 'cast your pearls before the swine.'"

Matthew 7:6

(read & chew)

Try to learn to play the guitar...it's easy. Use it in your personal worship. This is a picture of one I bought on E-bay and rebuilt for my son Thomas.

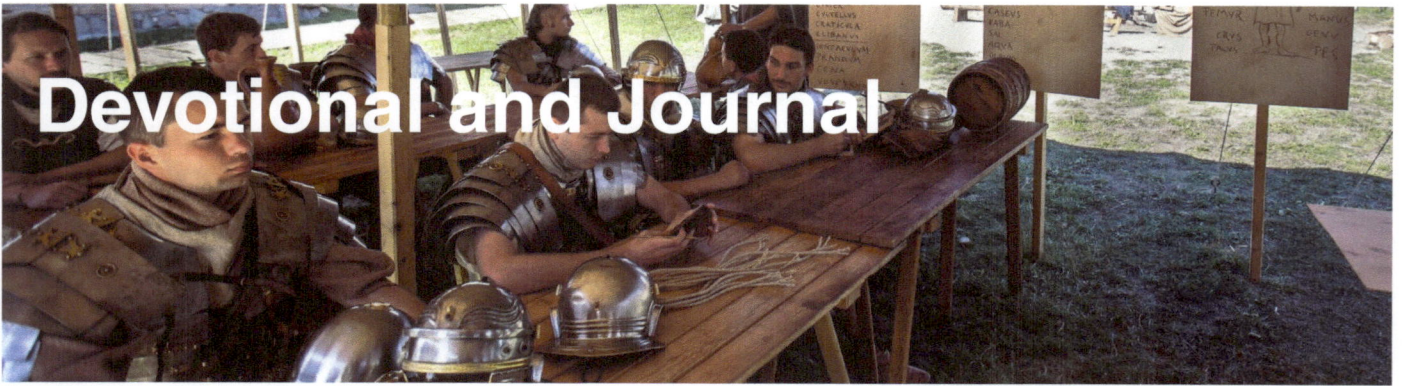

Devotional and Journal

Dear Gentlemen,

"But his delight is in the law of the Lord;
And in His law doth he meditate
day and night."

Psalm 1:2

(read & chew)

The Word of God is sweeter than a fine-looking woman... the beauty of the flesh will fade, droop, and wrinkle, but the Word of God will become more and more beautiful every day you get to know it. Do you crave it as you would the sweetest honey, or as the deer pants for the waters? The real believer craves the Words and teachings of Jesus Christ.

Christ is the baseline of all interpretation of all Scripture. The question for us is never, "how do you see it?", but rather, "how does Jesus see it?"

To do this, you must, as David did, meditate on His word day and night so that when you are not reading it, you are thinking about it; and when you are sleeping, you will dream about it!

Michelangelo claimed he could see the statue in the marble… He just removed rock that was in the way. Jesus sees your potential and died before He knew us!

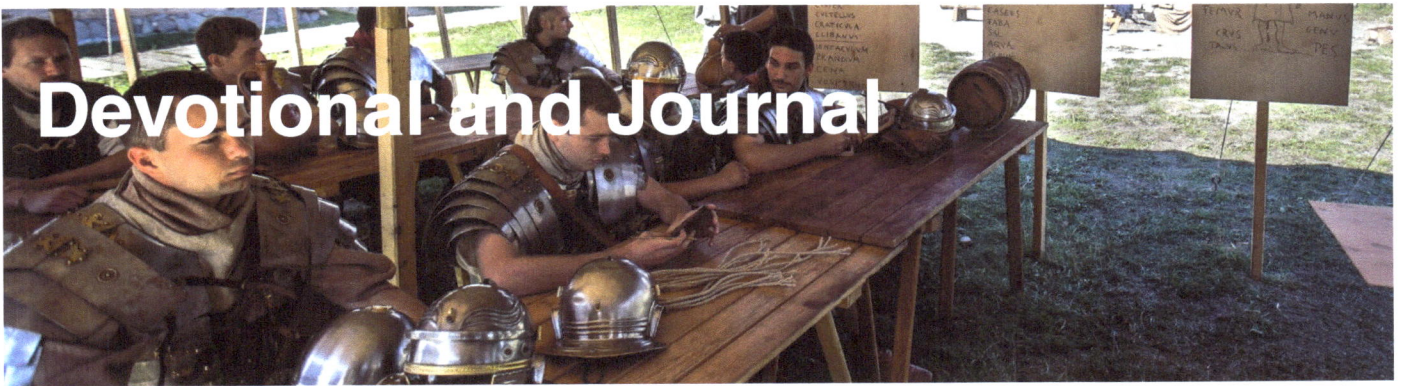

Devotional and Journal

Dear Gentlemen,

To be a man of integrity, you have to be a man whose ways don't vary from times of pressure to times of ease. In Psalm 1: 3, David teaches us that the man who is grounded in the Word of God is:

"Like a tree planted by the rivers of water that bringeth forth his fruit in his season, his leaf also shall not wither; And whatsoever he doeth shall prosper."

(read & chew)

A tree planted deep into the Word cannot be blown down or conveniently plowed away. Sink your roots men, into God's Word and glean His wisdom, and then make a determination in your heart to live by it. When you are like a tree that lives, dwells, and tabernacles with God's Word,

you will never spiritually "dry up."

I frequently have heard many a man say that he is going through a "dry spell." If that happens to you, dig your roots deeper into the Word of God till you hit the stream of life.

"But whoever drinks the water I give them will never thirst. Indeed, the water I give them will become in them a spring of water welling up to eternal life."

John 14:4

(read & chew)

"God will never plant the seed of His life upon the soil of a hard, unbroken spirit. He will only plant that seed where the conviction of His Spirit has brought brokenness, where the soil has been watered with the tears of repentance as well as the tears of joy."

Alan Redpath

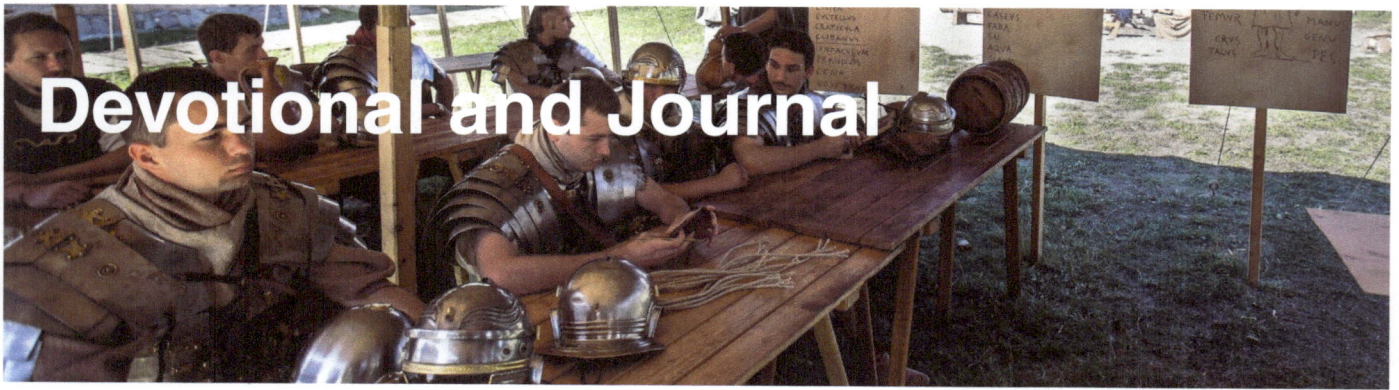

Devotional and Journal

Dear Gentlemen,

Psalm 1: 3b teaches you that if you are planted by the streams of water, your life (tree) will yield its fruit in season. Your life will find the purpose of God, and your ministries will produce regular seasonal fruit and you will not have dry periods. So he says that your leaves will never wither, but on the contrary, God will prosper you spiritually at whatever you lay your hands to. On the other hand, David is extremely clear—and not very politically correct, by today's standards—when he says in that:

Psalm 1:3-6:

The ungodly are not so: but are like the chaff which the wind drives away. Therefore the ungodly shall not stand in the judgment, nor sinners in the congregation of the righteous.
For the Lord knows the way of the righteous:
but the way of the ungodly shall perish.
(read & chew)

Think not about the "easy life" of the wicked, for God—He who is ultimately important—sees them like momentary chaff or dust in the wind. These men who reject God's Word and God's ways will not stand in the judgment of God, but will fall when it counts; they won't be able to stand with their "puffed up" pride next to you, who humbly wears the righteousness of Christ.

"David knew that all the question marks of his life were in the hand of God. He knew it was impossible to be in God's hand and in the enemy's hand at the same time. The gloom begins to disappear and fear departs as faith emerges in glorious triumph. This man is rising out of his testing and adversity to learn to put his utter dependence on the Lord."

– Alan Redpath,

The Making of a Man of God: Lessons from the Life of David

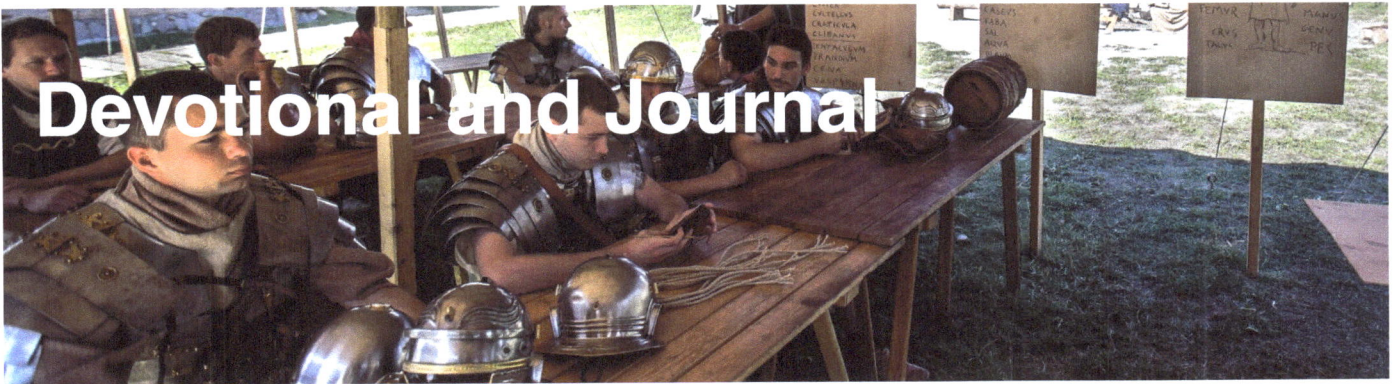

Devotional and Journal

Dear Gentlemen,

Psalm 1: 6

"For the Lord watches over the way of the righteous;
but the way of the ungodly (wicked) shall perish (lead to destruction)."

(read & chew)

Gentlemen, there are always choices for the believer. Prior to your salvation, you were slaves to sin and had no free will. Having been set free from sin, purchased and paid for in full by Jesus Christ, we are possessions of Christ, and our will has been set free. Jesus said it like this:
"... If you continue in My word, then you are My disciples indeed; and you shall know the Truth (His word), and the Truth shall set you free."

John 8:31 – 32

(read & chew)

He also said this based on His eternal nature: "whatever He makes free will be free indeed."

Use your freedom of will as an exercise in obedience to gain God's directions. When you come to the paths that fork into two directions, have it already settled in your heart that you're going to seek and to take the path of Christ. You will know that path as you know the "logos," the living Word who is Christ Jesus. Pray to God and read His Word. Then listen for His voice. Jesus will clarify your life and mission as you go in obedience into the entire world preaching, baptizing, and teaching (making disciples). Set your heart to always do the right thing in Christ! Take time to create a list of things which you have become aware of in the Scriptures that are the things you definitely know are God's will. This will save you a lot of time when a quick decision is needed.

"There is some task which the God of all the Universe, the Great Creator, your Redeemer in Jesus Christ has for you to do--and which will remain undone and incomplete until, by faith and obedience, you step into the will of God."

- Alan Redpath

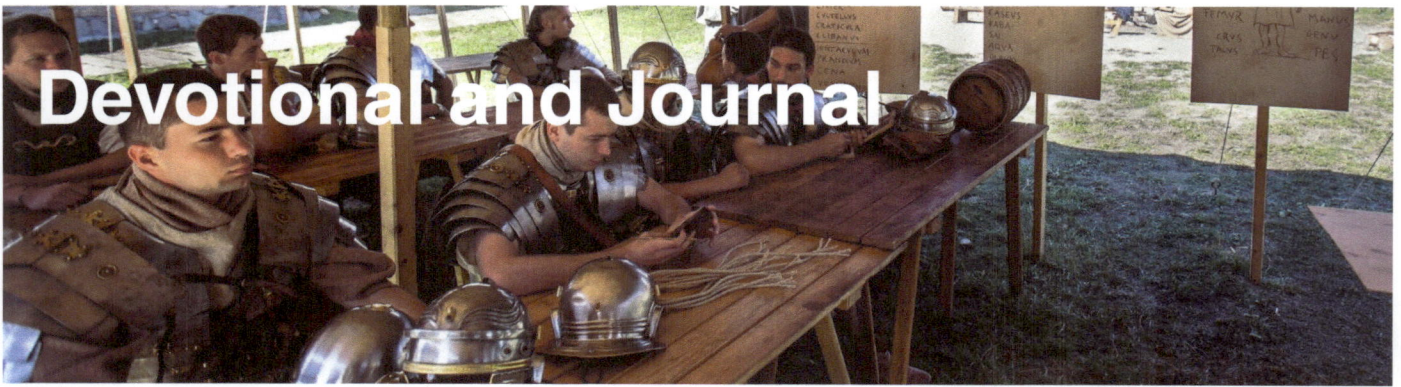

Gentlemen,

The only men that I know that don't like to fish are men who never had the joy of catching a good fish. I think that fishing or the "fishing bug," is probably going to be found by scientists to be in the DNA coding of every man someday! Every once in a while, it does a man's soul good to go fishing. Jesus had an affinity for fishermen and chose several of them to be his first recruits. He calls to each one of you today: "come and follow Me, and I will make you fishers of men." Sharing Christ with others is in your God-given DNA.

It's easy because it's natural... Just like fishing.
Not fishing is unnatural! (Tell this to your wife).
God is giving you permission to fish for men.
When you catch your first "big one," your life will never be the same!

Matthew 4:18-22 says:

"As Jesus was walking beside the sea of Galilee, He saw two brothers, Simon called Peter and his brother Andrew. They were casting a net into the lake, for they were fishermen. "Come follow me," Jesus said, "and I will send you out to fish for people." At once they left their nets and followed Him. Going on from there, He saw two other brothers, James son of Zebedee, and his brother John. They were in the boat with their father Zebedee, preparing their nets. Jesus called them, and immediately they left the boat and their father and followed Him.

Read and chew

> "The conversion of a soul is the miracle of a moment, but the manufacture of a saint is the task of a lifetime."
>
> *Alan Redpath*

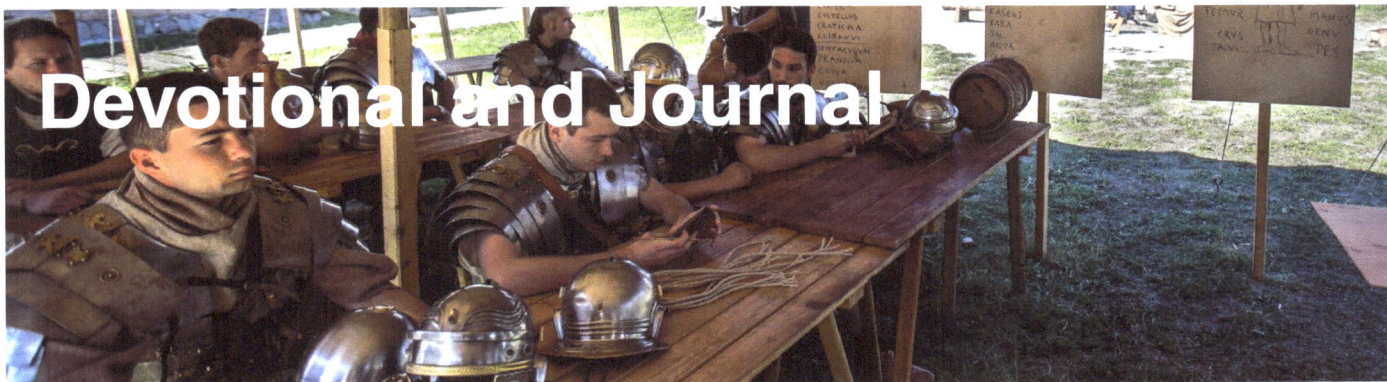

Devotional and Journal

Dear Gentlemen,

When the boys were little, we lived in two disaster areas. In Southern California, we lived in an area that was under the threat of huge fires. The fires crossed the mountains and were whipped up by the 70 mile-per-hour Santa Ana winds. If the fires got close, we would have to evacuate our home. If the fires approached quickly, we would have to choose a few items of value and leave the area with our family without hesitation. Mom and I had a pre-plan as to what we would take with us.

Heaven can come upon us in an instant. Once we are there, we can't reach back for the people we have left behind. Consider each day who you want to take with you to escape the fire. Make a covenant in your heart to leave no loved one behind. Consider the plight of the man in the story in:

Luke 12: 20

"But God said to him, 'You fool! This very night your life will be demanded from you. Then who will get what you have prepared for yourself?

You fool! This very night your soul is required of you...'"

(read & chew)

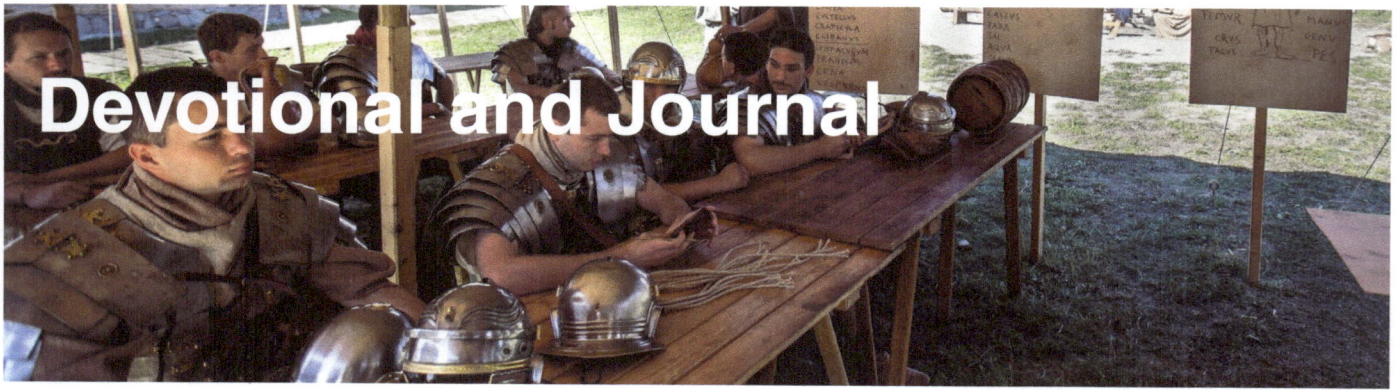

Devotional and Journal

Dear Gentlemen,

Isaiah 52:7 says,

"How beautiful on the mountains are the feet of those who bring good news, who proclaim peace, who bring good tidings, who proclaim salvation, who say to Zion, 'your God reigns.'"

(read & chew)

Mountains in the Scriptures usually are the representation of nations, or in this case, the nation of Israel. When we share Christ with a lost and dying world, we bring a "right" relationship to the people; we bring salvation to lost and hurting people. At this point, the people then have the blinders of sin removed from their eyes and can shout, "Our God reigns!" When one sinner repents and turns to God the Bible teaches us that:

the angels in heaven rejoice.

Luke 15:7 – 10

(read & chew)

Hurting people rejoice when you are an instrument of God's grace through your sharing of Christ with them.

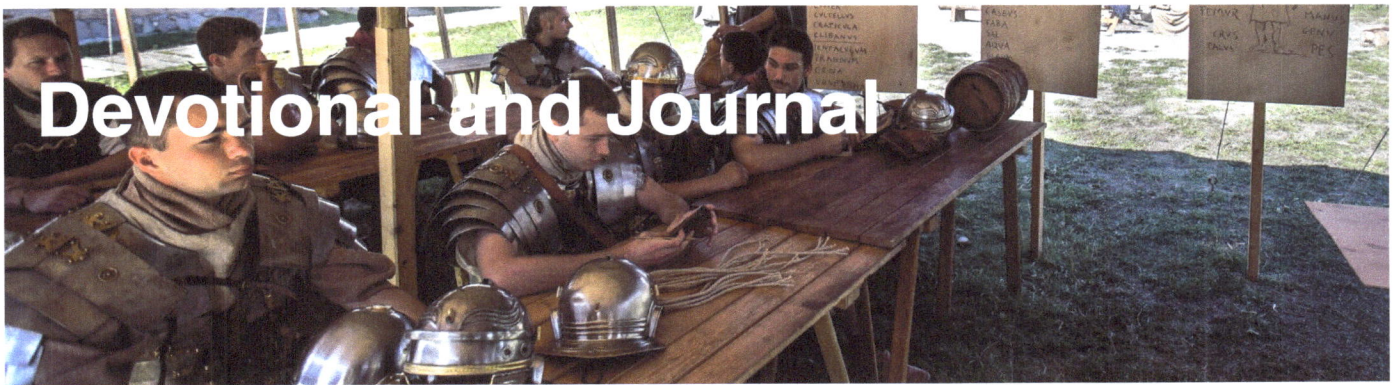

Devotional and Journal

Dear Gentlemen,

You're not here in this world to win a popularity contests. Jesus taught us in John 15:8 – 25

18 "If the world hates you, keep in mind that it hated Me first. 19 If you belonged to the world, it would love you as its own. As it is, you do not belong to the world, but I have chosen you out of the world. That is why the world hates you. 20 Remember what I told you: 'A servant is not greater than his master.' If they persecuted Me, they will persecute you also. If they obeyed My teaching, they will obey yours also. 21 They will treat you this way because of My name, for they do not know the One who sent Me. 22 If I had not come and spoken to them, they would not be guilty of sin; but now they have no excuse for their sin. 23 Whoever hates Me hates my Father as well. 24 If I had not done among them the works no one else did, they would not be guilty of sin. As it is, they have seen, and yet they have hated both Me and my Father. 25 But this is to fulfill what is written in their Law: 'They hated Me without reason.'

(read & chew)

If you preach Jesus and real salvation, the world at large will hate, despise, and persecute you. Fishing for men will not make you popular in Satan's kingdom. As you whittle away at the evil one's ranks, those who are lovers of evil will hate you. Oftentimes, a "trophy" fish will put up an amazing fight...expect this. The harder they resist, the more you must increase your efforts. Once hooked, this fish will eventually tire out and succumb to the fisherman's persistence. Remember in the book of Acts Chapter 2, verses 36-41, everyone that came to know Christ on that day (Pentecost) rejoiced, but just weeks before that, they were yelling at Christ: "Crucify Him, Crucify Him."

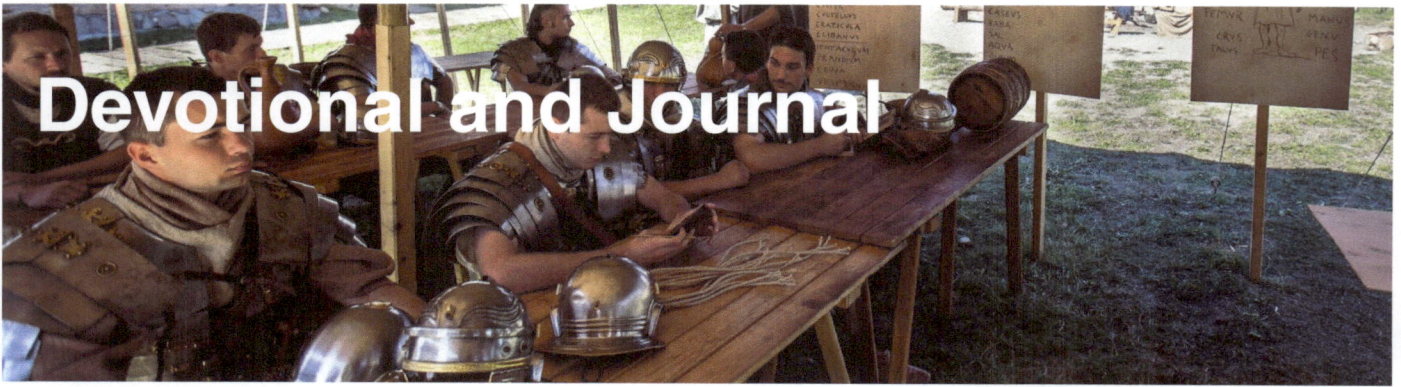

Devotional and Journal

Dear Gentlemen,

Acts 5:20, says

"...he said, 'Go and stand in the temple courts and tell the people all about this new Life.'"

(read & chew)

If you commit your life to sharing Christ whenever the opportunity presents itself, as long as you remain "in Christ," God will pull you out of Satan's attempts to shut you up. You must have a pre-set mindset, as the apostles did in Acts 5:29, that you are determined always to obey God over man. In the world, some will always be there to demand that you do not share Christ publicly or in their presence. Some people will say to you that if you talk about Jesus, they will not be your friend—but that is just the fight of a man being caught. Do not cave in to their threats. Gentlemen, friends do not let friends die and go to hell! Would you walk away from a man getting ready to jump to his death off of a high-rise? What if he said mean things to you? Fish hard gentlemen—and don't quit.

"There is nothing—no circumstance, no trouble, no testing—that can ever touch me until, first of all, it has gone past God and past Christ, right through to me. If it has come that far, it has come with a great purpose, which I may not understand at the moment. But as I refuse to become panicky—as I lift up my eyes to Him—and as I accept it as coming from the throne of God for some great purpose of blessing to my heart, no sorrow will ever disturb me, no trial will ever disarm me, no circumstance will cause me to fret—for I shall rest in the joy of what my Lord is. That is the rest of victory."

Alan Redpath

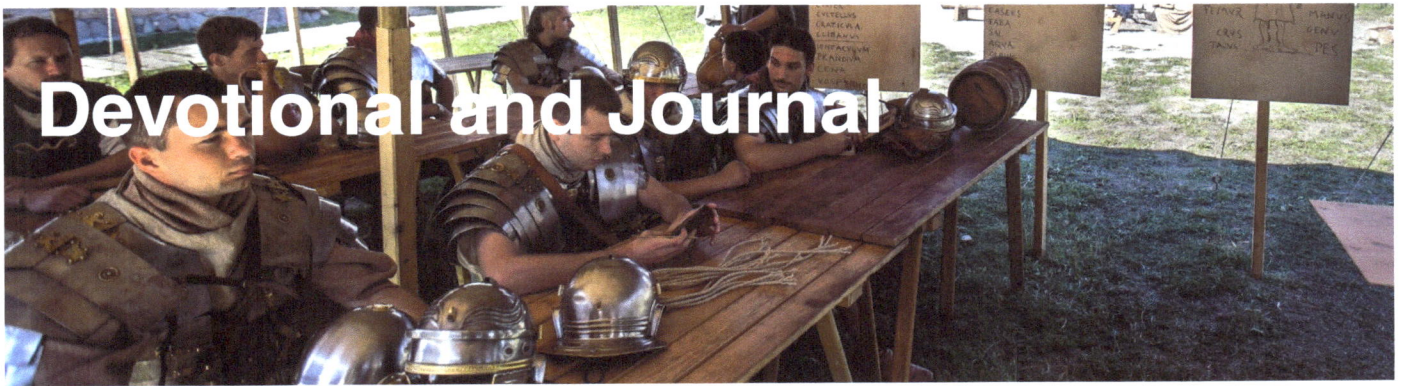

Devotional and Journal

Dear Gentlemen,

Today I want to share with you a fishing principal. I call it: The Principle Of The Last Place They Heard The Truth. Many times when you are sharing Christ with someone, they will get offended and angry. They will often say horrible things to you or about you, and sometimes they may even strike you or hurt you. But remember these words in those times:

Luke 6:22– 28

"Blessed are you when people hate you, when they exclude you and insult you and reject your name as evil, because of the Son of Man. Rejoice in that day and leap for joy, because great is your reward in heaven. For that is how their ancestors treated the prophets. But woe to you who are rich, for you have already received your comfort. Woe to you who are well fed now, for you will go hungry. Woe to you who laugh now, for you will mourn and weep. Woe to you when everyone speaks well of you, for that is how their ancestors treated the false prophets. But to you who are listening I say:

Love your enemies, do good to those who hate you, bless those who curse you, pray for those who mistreat you."

(read & chew)

This passage tells us not to be surprised when we are persecuted. Tell the truth of the gospel anyway. If the person leaves and is angry, pray for them and let God deal with them, but do not compromise God's truth for the appeasement of their anger. If you hold firm and don't quit or retaliate, at some point in the future that person will come to a crossroads in their life where they need God, and they will return to the last place they heard the truth.

Hopefully it will be you!

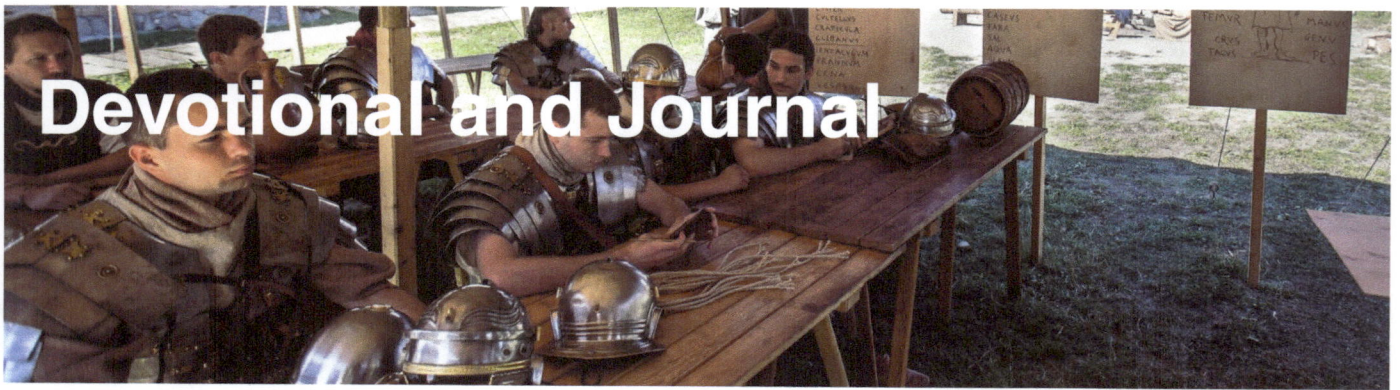

Dear Gentlemen,

"This is to My father's glory, that you bear much fruit, showing yourselves to be My disciples."

(read & chew)

The fruit that Jesus is talking about is souls that have been won to Christ. Notice here that Jesus has something quantitative in mind... Much fruit. This concept parallels the parable of the talents which requires a quantitative outcome from the gifts, which God has entrusted you, both in the realm of abilities and finances.

(Luke 19:11 – 27)

11 While they were listening to this, He went on to tell them a parable, because He was near Jerusalem and the people thought that the kingdom of God was going to appear at once. 12 He said: "A man of noble birth went to a distant country to have himself appointed king and then to return. 13 So he called ten of his servants and gave them ten minas. 'Put this money to work,' he said, 'until I come back.' 14 But his subjects hated him and sent a delegation after him to say, 'We don't want this man to be our king.' 15 He was made king, however, and returned home. Then he sent for the servants to whom he had given the money, in order to find out what they had gained with it. 16 The first one came and said, 'Sir, your mina has earned ten more.' 17 'Well done, my good servant!' his master replied. 'Because you have been trustworthy in a very small matter, take charge of ten cities.' 18 The second came and said, 'Sir, your mina has earned five more.' 19 His master answered, 'You take charge of five cities.' 20 Then another servant came and said, 'Sir, here is your mina; I have kept it laid away in a piece of cloth. 21 I was afraid of you, because you are a hard man. You take out what you did not put in and reap what you did not sow.' 22 His master replied, 'I will judge you by your own words, you wicked servant! You knew, did you, that I am a hard man, taking out what I did not put in, and reaping what I did not sow? 23 Why then didn't you put my money on deposit, so that when I came back, I could have collected it with interest?' 24 Then he said to those standing by, 'Take his mina away from him and give it to the one who has ten minas.' 25 'Sir,' they said, 'he already has ten!' 26 He replied, 'I tell you that to everyone who has, more will be given, but as for the one who has nothing, even what they have will be taken away. 27 But those enemies of mine who did not want me to be king over them—bring them here and kill them in front of me.'"

It is not for someone else in the ethereal "out there" to be the soul winner, or the fisherman. It is for every true disciple. The idea that you can be a disciple of Christ and ignore His prime directive given in the Great Commission is foreign to the Word of God.

In this area of Christianity, many people are deceiving themselves; let it not be you! Go...Fish...

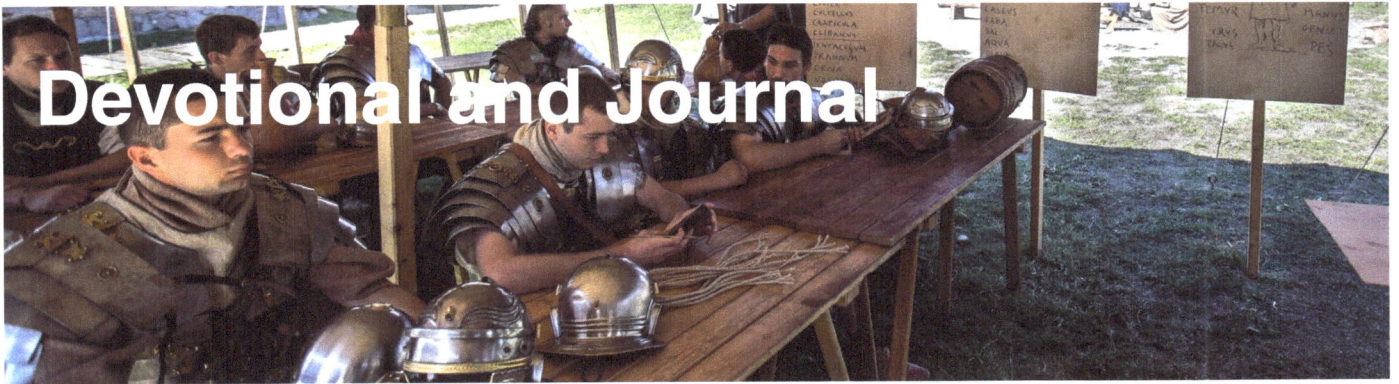

Devotional and Journal

Gentlemen,

Hebrews 11:6

"And without faith it is impossible to please God, because anyone who comes to Him must believe that He exists and that He rewards those who earnestly seek Him."

(read & chew)

Your faith in God belongs to you. With your faith, you can go through this life and make a profound difference to all those around you. Faith is the possession of the knowledge that God exists and is alive and in control of all, and that He seeks a relationship with us. Real faith is a possession that cannot be shaken or lost. Real faith says, "I bet my life, my all on God."

Real faith believes like one's life depends on it; that when Jesus says if we believe in Him, we too, will surely be resurrected like Him. Real faith believes it can move mountains with the Christ in me! Mountains and Scriptures are allusions to nations. Real faith believes we can move nations. For this reason I still believe we can make a difference in ours.

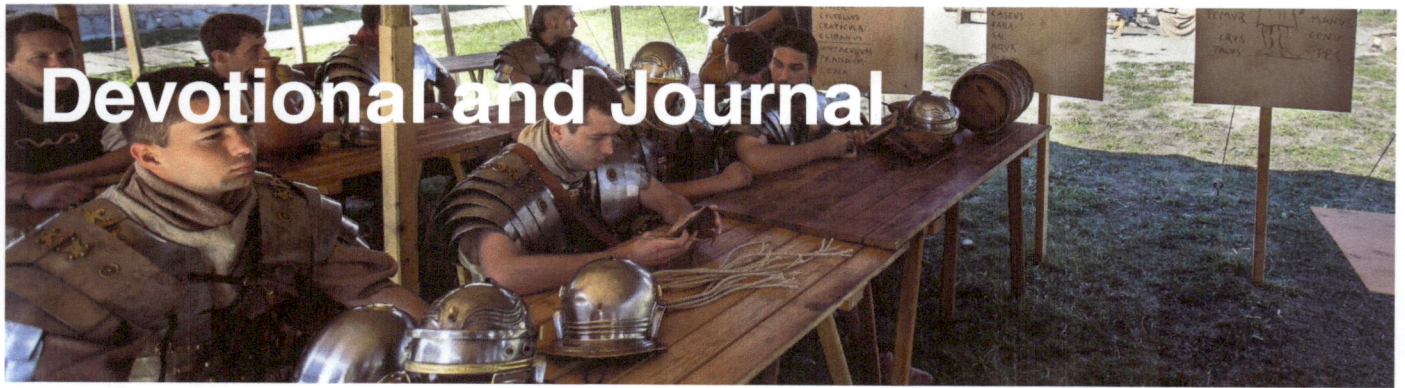

Dear Gentlemen,

As Jesus spoke of the end times, He tells us that at that time many will turn away from the faith and will betray and hate each other. One of the great things we as men can give to the world is to be men of faith. The kind of man whose hope is in God and cannot be moved or shaken; he stands out in sharp contrast to the "politically correct" wimps of today. Over time, as your faith proves to be consistent, the world who once mocked you will come to respect you and your God. A man who wins at faith is considered trustworthy. **The people of the world, in fact, are craving true heroes in the back of their minds; the people are hoping that out there somewhere, there are still real men who truly display Biblical faith. Be that man!**

Romans 1:8

"I am not ashamed of the gospel of Christ, for it is the power of God unto salvation; first for the Jew and then for the Gentile."

(read & chew)

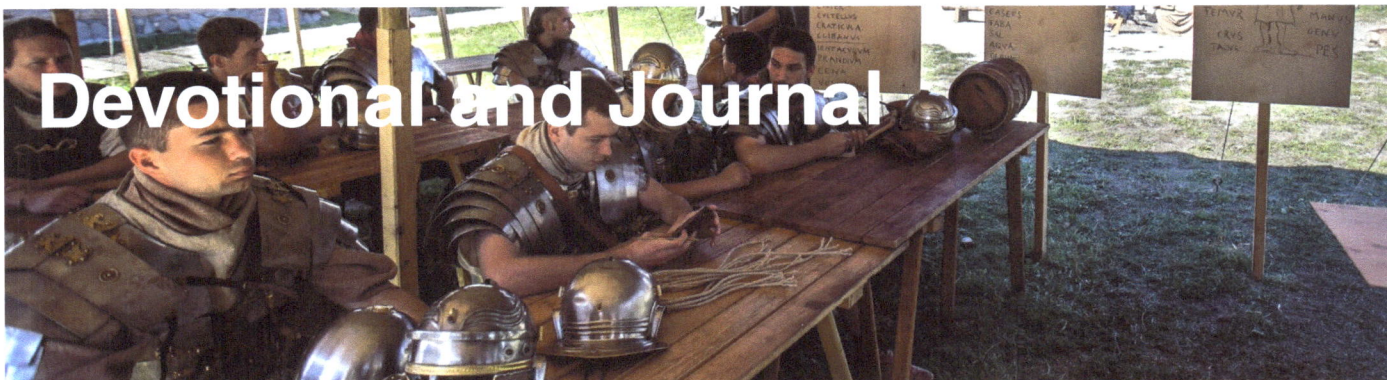

Devotional and Journal

Dear Gentlemen,

When faced with the force of what Jesus was asking the disciples to do, they asked Jesus, "increase our faith." Luke 17:5 (read & chew)

Faith is a variable, but any time we feel weak in our faith, we can go to God and ask Him to increase our faith. God knows our weaknesses, and that many times our faith is not where it needs to be. We can all recognize when our faith is low, so let's ask God to increase our faith. I have noticed a formula in the Bible for increasing our faith. Throughout the Bible, people increased their faith by recounting the finished works of God throughout history. Those seeking more faith will recount all the miracles and acts of God, both in the Bible and in our lives. My grandfather Myers gave to me a faith heritage. When I was young, he had a music box that held Scripture memory verses. The box also contained a music machine harp. When wound up, it played an old hymn of the faith entitled: "Standing On The Promises." He would sing the words to me in is whispery, elderly voice.

In 1879 Russell Kelso Carter, who had lived a full young life as a teacher and a coach, was diagnosed with an untreatable heart condition. Russell knelt down and promised God that whether healed or not, he would serve God for the rest of his life—no matter what. There beside his bed, he consecrated his life to God. The written Word came alive for him and he began to stand on God's promises for his life and healing. He determined to fully place his faith in God no matter what. Go ahead and read tomorrow's lesson, and spend two days on the impact of this song.

Dear Gentlemen,

The day that I received word my grandfather Myers died, the hundred and fifty voice men's choir at Southwestern seminary made a circle around me, and in four-part harmony sang the song: "Standing On The Promises." As you read the words this great hymn of the faith, I want you to internalize the principles from the song and make them part of your heart. You are welcome to look up the tune on the net so that you can sing too.

verse 1.

Standing on the promises of Christ my King, through eternal ages let His praises ring,
Glory in the Highest, I will shout and sing;
Standing on the promises of God.

Chorus:

Standing, standing,
Standing on the promises
of Christ, my Savior.
Standing, standing
Standing on the promises of God.

verse 2.

Standing on the promises that cannot fail, when the howling storms of doubt and fear avail.
By the living Word of God, I shall prevail; Standing on the promises of God.

verse 3.

Standing on the promises I now can see,
New perfect, present cleansing in the Blood for me.
Standing in the liberty
when Christ makes me free;
Standing on the promises of God.

verse 4.

Standing on the promises of Christ, the Lord,
Bound to Him eternally by love's strong cord,
Overcoming daily with the Spirits Sword;
Standing on the promises of God.

verse 5.

Standing on the promises I cannot fail, Listening every moment to the spirits call, Resting in my Savior as my all in all;
Standing on the promises of God.

Make a list of God's interventions in your life and stand on them. Share them with your family and your church, and watch your faith grow!

"God's call to any man and the anointing of the Spirit for service are conditioned upon that man's heart response."

- Alan Redpath

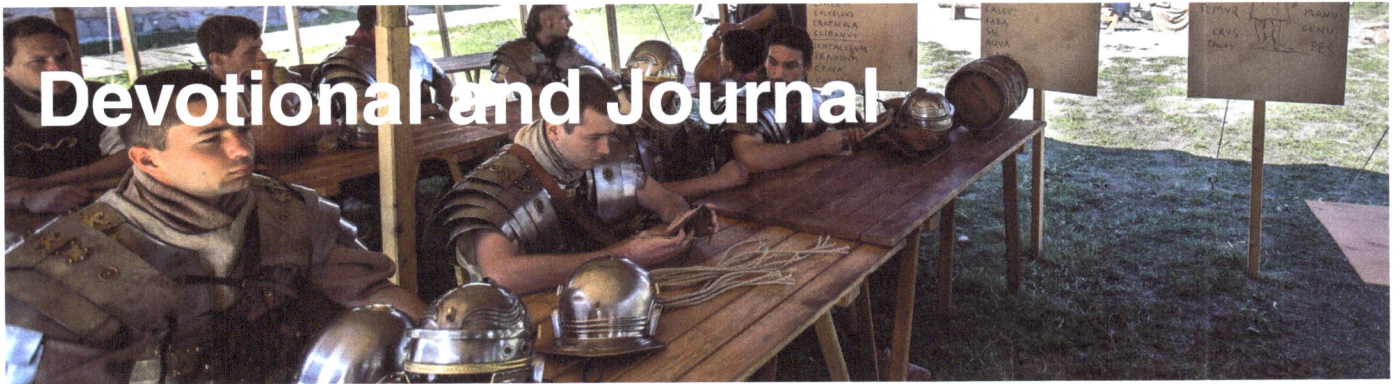

Devotional and Journal

Dear Gentlemen,

It is my heart's desire that you understand the principle that
Martin Luther cried out against the religious system:

"...the just shall live by faith!"

Romans, 1:17

(read & chew)

Faith is not something we put on for the church on the weekends. Faith is something we have to learn to live by. Faith means that you will always lean on God's arms as if He is there holding you up like a little boy on a bike for the first time. Faith is: knowing that your daddy has you, should you fall. Your sovereign God is fully aware of your flaws and is never surprised by your falling; and so He is there to catch you and to help you regain your confidence...and get back on the bike. God can handle a man who falls, but He cannot handle a man who falls and refuses to get back on the bike.

1 John, 1:9

If we confess our sins, He is faithful and just and will forgive us our sins and purify us from all unrighteousness.

(read & chew)

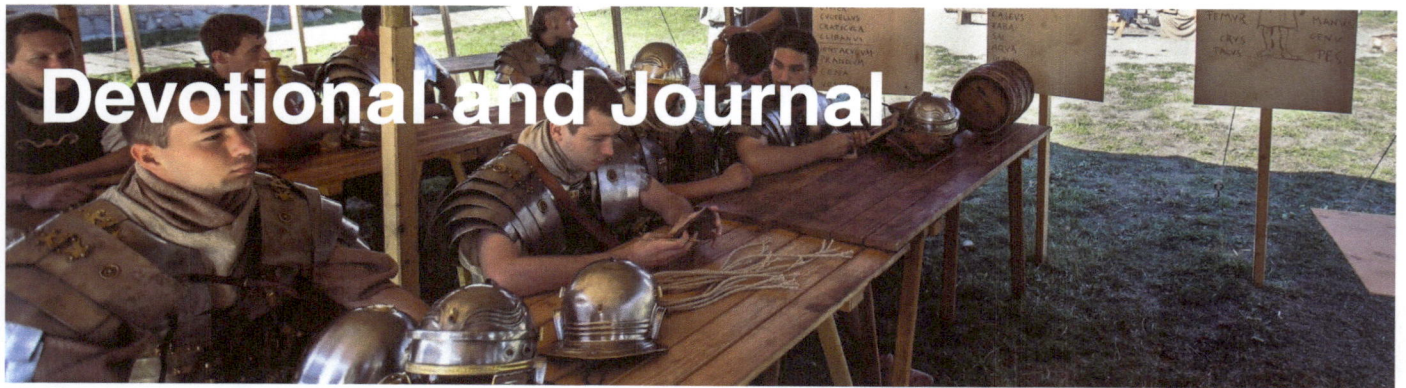

Devotional and Journal

Dear Gentlemen,

"...But I have prayed for you, that your faith fails not."
Luke 22: 32

(read & chew)

Whenever you fall, commit in your heart to get up and go back to work in Christ's Kingdom. I call this the "Peter Principle." Jesus knew Peter would lead the failure of all the disciples. Jesus reinstated Peter after the resurrection and told him to get back to the prime directive.

He does the same with you when you fall. The best thing you can do if you stumble is to immediately repent and return to God's mission—remember, believe that God is. Stop treating Him as if He merely has the intelligence of a very brilliant person. He is God—Master Creator of the World and of all knowledge. Get up, clean off your shield of faith and go back into the battle formation!

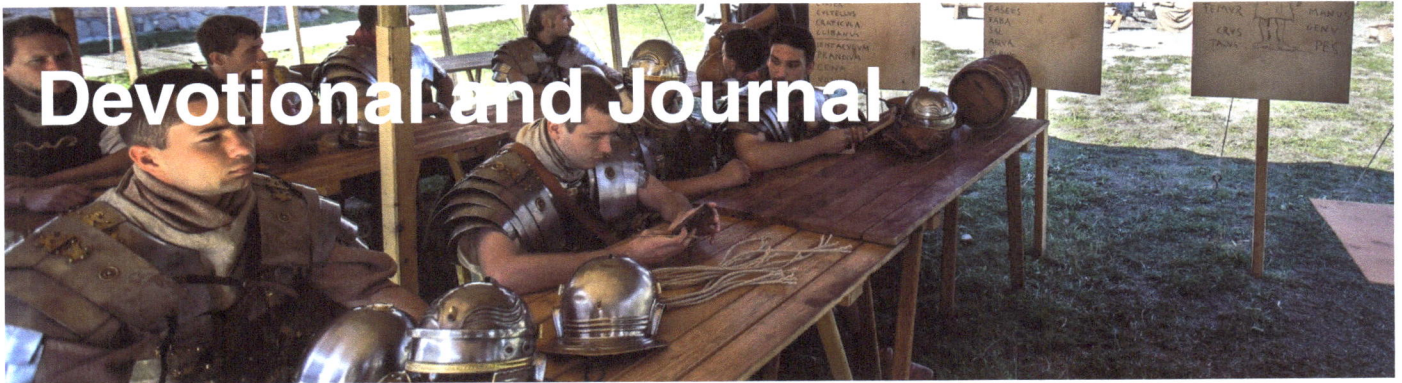

Devotional and Journal

Dear Gentlemen,

1st Timothy 6: 10 – 14

"For the love of money is the root of all kinds of evil;
and by craving it, some have wandered away from the faith
and pierced themselves with many pains. . ."

(read & chew)

Trusting in money can quickly take the place of trusting in God. Craving it quickly puts $$$$$ on the throne. Jesus said, due to His understanding of human nature, that you cannot serve two masters: God and money; you will love the one and hate the other. Paul tells Timothy here to run from this issue, and instead to refocus his thoughts on pursuing righteousness, godliness, faith, love, endurance and gentleness. In verse 12 he tells Timothy to

fight the good fight for faith!

(read & chew)

This means that you're going to have to fight
to keep faith at the highest level in your life...

"Faith is two empty hands held open to receive all of the Lord."

- Alan Redpath

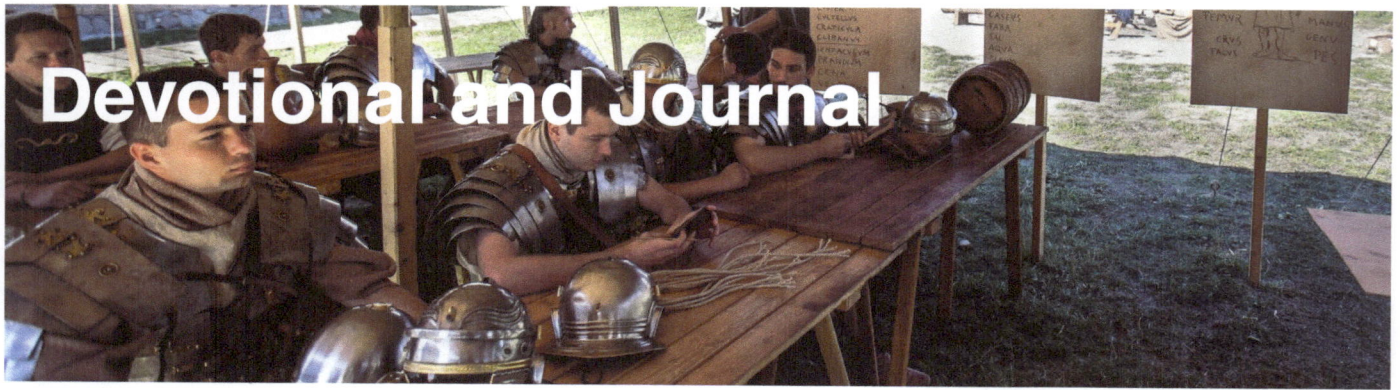

Gentlemen,

For some reason, my father always loved talking about salt, or teaching me about salt. He loved to prepare a big piece of steak by rubbing salt into it as he told me how the salt would eventually migrate through the meat into every cell. He would then talk about how the salt flavors, purifies, and preserves the meat. He would then turn to me and say, "Rob, never lose your salty tang." When salt loses its abilities to perform these functions, it becomes useless.

"How can I be salt?," I would ask. My dad, then, would look at me and say, "You are like salt. Jesus wants you to penetrate the world with your flavor, with healing, with purity, and with preservation. Think about it like this: you are the missing ingredient that Jesus Christ has prepared for all the areas of life that you touch: at home, at work, and even in your neighborhood."

So today, ask yourself the question:

How can I penetrate my world with my salt?

Matthew 5:13

You are the salt of the earth. But if the salt loses its saltiness, how can it be made salty again? It is no longer good for anything, except to be thrown out and trampled underfoot.

(read & chew)

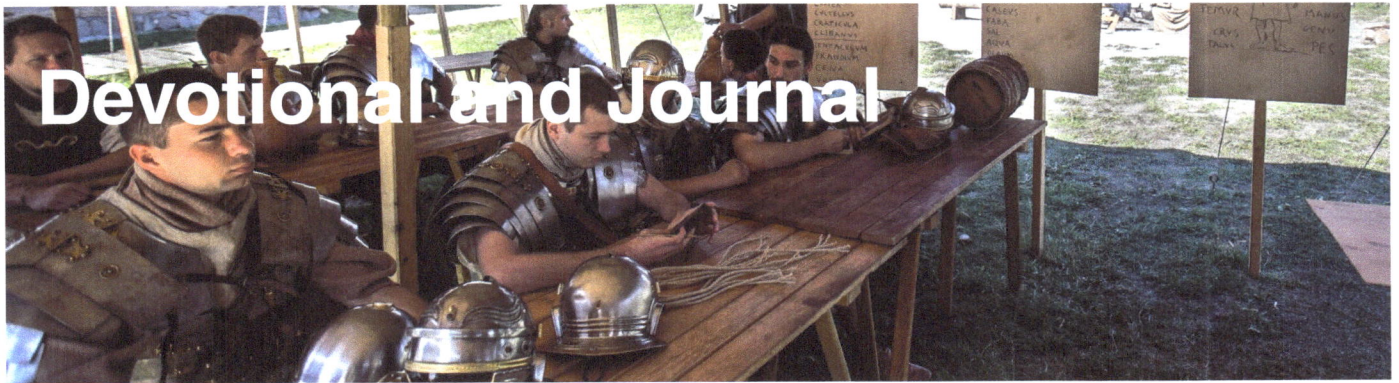

Devotional and Journal

Gentlemen,

Salt is about leadership. Jesus washed the feet to demonstrate a leadership style that He wanted us, His disciples, to implement. His teaching on leadership was the opposite of how the world approaches leadership, both then and now. It is interesting to see that in most of Christendom, the "servant" leadership style that Jesus purported declined to a state of nonexistence within 100 years after His death.

Even today, most churches just pay "lip-service" to the style of servant leadership. Washing feet means that, as a leader, I have to not just be willing to get down and dirty in service, but that I have to lead by the example of being the first to serve. Notice how the Apostles then, and pastors today, do not fight to be the first to gain this privilege. Jesus had a leadership problem that had to do with men who saw leadership as a power position. In Christ, therefore, leadership is not about the power to control, but of the blessing it is to serve others.

John 13:14-17:

"Now that I, Your Lord and Teacher, have washed your feet, you also should wash one another's feet. I have set you an example that you should do as I have done for you. Very truly I tell you, no servant is greater than his master, nor is a messenger greater than the one who sent him. Now that you know these things, you will be blessed if you do them."

(read & chew)

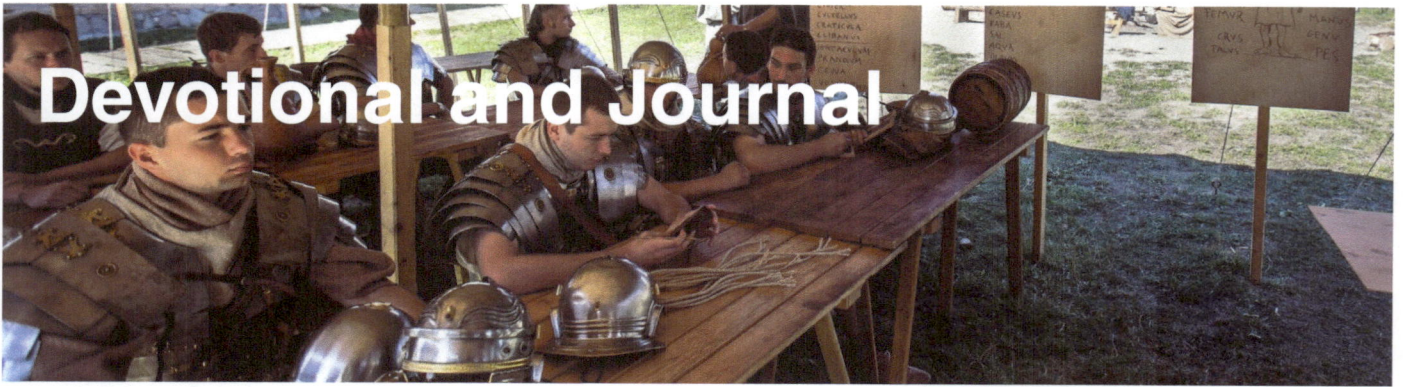

Dear Gentlemen,

John 13:1-17 (re-read & chew more)

"Now that I, your Lord and Teacher, have washed your feet, you also should wash one another's feet. I have set you an example that you should do as I have done for you. Very truly I tell you, no servant is greater than his master, nor is a messenger greater than the one who sent him. Now that you know these things, you will be blessed if you do them." [red]

A man with real salt is a man who says what he means, and means what he says. He is a man whose word purifies the world. Salt in a wound cleans the wound by killing the bacteria. Salt sometimes stings, but we make the world a better place when we purify it. This is about integrity. We must be people who can be counted on, who set the tone as the best workers, the hardest fighters, and the most loyal friends. When we lose our salty tang, the world says that we are not worth our salt. John Maxwell, the Christian leadership guru, says that, "integrity is what you are when nobody else is looking." I add to this the concept that integrity is also what you are, when everybody is looking.

The two applications are this:

1. Make a decision to do the right thing even when no one is watching.

2. Make a decision to do the right thing, and not change your principles to be politically correct in front of a crowd.

"Integrity is what you are when nobody else is looking..."

John Maxwell

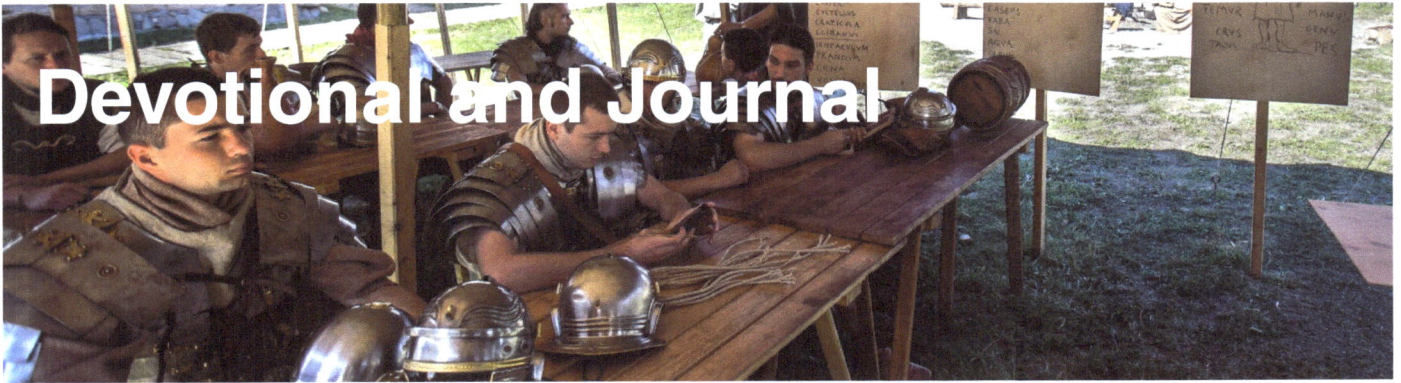

Devotional and Journal

Dear Gentlemen,

Many of you desire to be good leaders in your home. There is no such thing as a person who is a parent, but not a leader. Homes are designed to have leaders. The fact of the matter is that every home has one of two types of leaders. Home leaders are either good leaders or bad leaders, because whether you like it or not, if you are the man in your home, your family is relegated for a good part of your life to follow you wherever you go, and to be impacted by whatever you choose to do. Jesus tells us in Matthew 20: 25-28, that we are not to lead like the Gentiles who command and control from the top down, but we are to lead by serving the least first.

Don't try to lead in the church until you master serving in the world.

"Jesus called them together and said, 'You know that the rulers of the Gentiles lord it over them, and their high officials exercise authority over them. Not so with you. Instead, whoever wants to become great among you must be your servant, 27 and whoever wants to be first must be your slave—just as the Son of Man did not come to be served, but to serve, and to give His life as a ransom for many.'"

Matthew 20: 25-28

(read & chew)

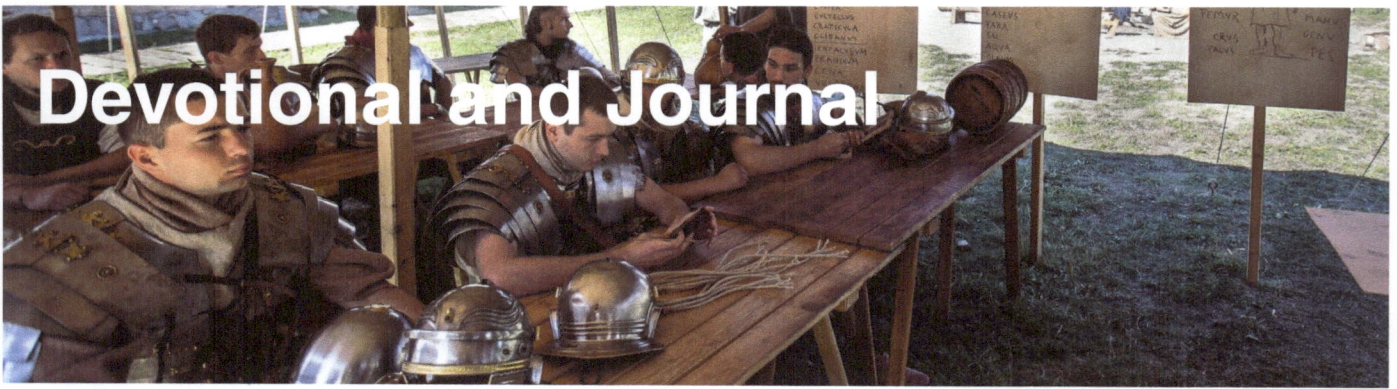

Dear Gentlemen,

In the days of old, salt was used to punish and control conquered nations. The conquering army would enslave the people and then salt the land to destroy it by making it barren for generations. The salt has an herbicidal effect similar to the herbicide "Round Up." The conquered people would accept their lot as slaves because they knew that their land could not support life if they returned. It was part of the psychological warfare.

There are many stories of brave men who sealed their fate by destroying their escape routes. One such example can be found in the story of the men of the Alamo, who could have escaped their deaths and left the prize of San Antonio without a fight, before Santa Anna's huge Mexican Army arrived. Fort Commander William Travis drew a line in the dust with his sword and asked every man that would step across that line to commit to fight to the death for the freedom of Texas. To be a disciple of Christ, you have to salt the desires of this world and commit with your life to the battle for the Gospel of the Christ!

"But if serving the Lord seems undesirable to you, then choose for yourselves this day whom you will serve, whether the gods your ancestors served beyond the Euphrates, or the gods of the Amorites, in whose land you are living. But as for me and my household, we will serve the Lord."

Joshua 24:15

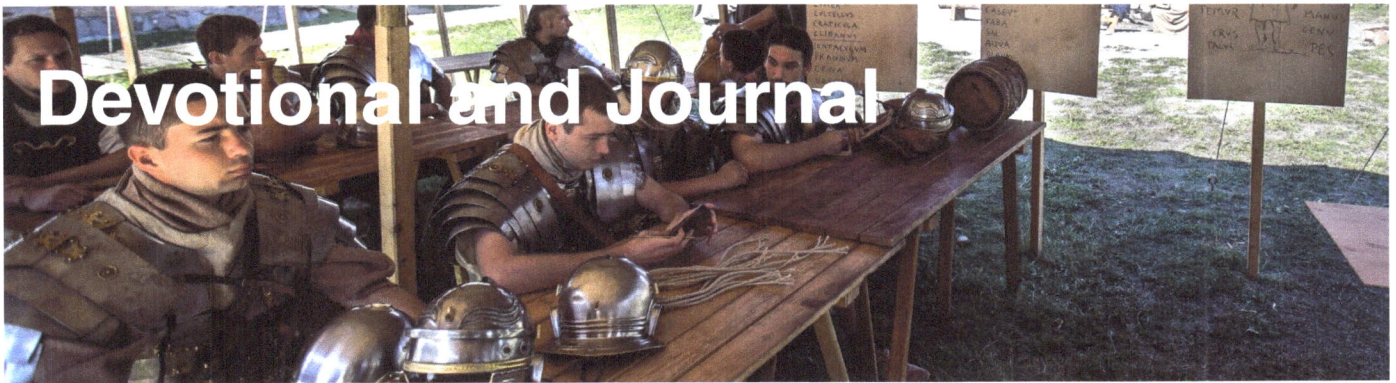

Devotional and Journal

Dear Gentlemen,

The application I have for you today is to apply salt to your past life. Salt all the "misdeeds of the flesh." Depart from fond memories of past sins. Destroy the things that Satan uses to get you down. Salt them! Kill those bad memories!

Paul said it like this in Philippians 3:

"...but one thing I do: Forgetting what is behind and straining toward what is ahead, I press on toward the goal to win the prize for which God has called me heavenward in Christ Jesus."

(read & chew)

Salt the earth; kick out the crutches of things
from the past away from your straight path.
Don't ever return, and don't entertain the thoughts.
Focus on what is ahead, and walk in Him!

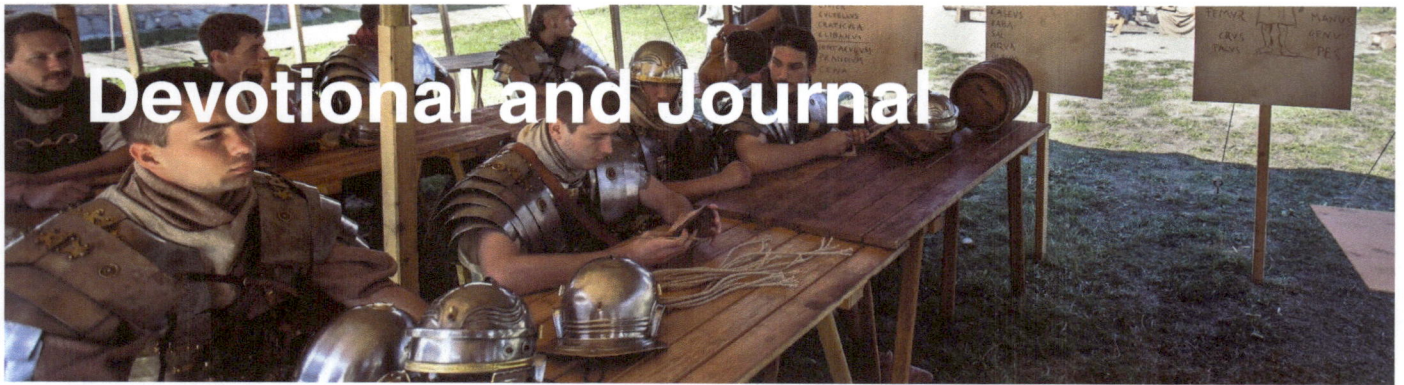

Devotional and Journal

Gentlemen,

You must set a new standard as to what Christian leadership looks like! The world does not recognize Jesus in many of the high-profile leaders of today. If you were to take a tour of the Capital of the United States and read the documents of the greatest men of our nation, you would see that this great nation of ours was founded by men who had a personal relationship with Jesus Christ.

Borrowing from track and field, we place the crossbar of our leadership high, where God initially placed it—not in the mud inches off the ground where any man can crawl through.

In our time, as in Romans 1:18,

"many men suppress the truth of God by their unrighteousness."

It is time... It is time for us to rise up! Presbyterian pastor William Merrill wrote this great hymn for his large men's ministry in New York City. A few years ago in the Los Angeles Coliseum, I heard over 100,000 men sing the song over 5 miles away from the stadium. It is an interesting fact that I could hear the voices of the men but not the instruments accompanying them. It was beautiful.

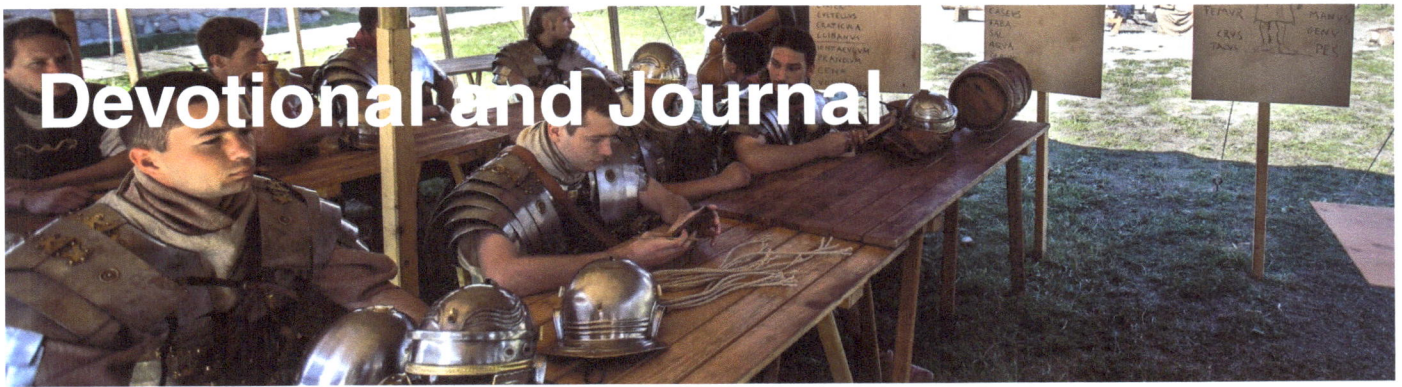

Continued

The song is entitled:
"Rise Up, Oh Men Of God"

Bring in the day of brotherhood,
And end the night of wrong.

Rise up, oh men of God!
The church for you doth wait;
Her strengths unequal to her task;
Rise up and make her great!

Rise up, oh men of God!
Have done with lesser things,
Give heart and soul
and mind and strength,
to serve the King of Kings.

Lift high the Cross of Christ!
Tread where His feet have trod;
As brothers of the Son of Man,
Rise Up, oh men of God!

Rise up, oh men of God!
His Kingdom tarries long,

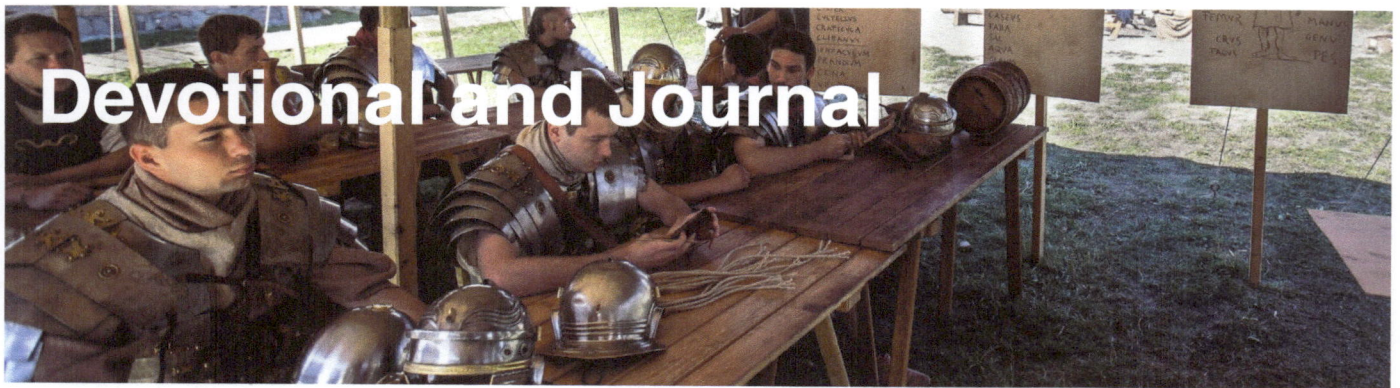

Dear Gentlemen,

Jesus said,

"This is my commandment,
that you love one another as I have loved you."

John 15:12

(read & chew)

Jesus breaks the roles of the macho stereotype and tells His men... no.

He also demands that His disciples not only like each other, but that they unconditionally love each other as well. The love He commands is unconditional / unselfish love; it is a love that lays down its life for a friend!

This agape love is not an option. Jesus teaches us the two great Commandments are centered in this love: to love your God with all your heart, soul, and mind... And if you really love God in this manner, you will love what God sees as valuable: the people He died for. If we love God, we will love what He loves: People.

"...He that does not love does not know God."

1 John 4:7-8

Dear friends, let us love one another, for love comes from God. Everyone who loves has been born of God and knows God. Whoever does not love does not know God, because God is love.

(read & chew)

Devotional and Journal

Gentlemen,

1st John 4:17 says:

"Herein is our love made perfect, that we may have boldness in the day of judgment, because as He is, so are we in this world."

(read & chew)

God wants your life to be full of His love for you, and in the security of your salvation, so that you won't have any worries in the day of judgment; you will be able to walk into His presence boldly and pick up your crown, as a prince or brother to the king! The resulting fact of His love will be that we will have "no fear in judgment, for perfect love casts off fear!"(vs. 18)

What amazing peace we have, my brothers, in the love of Christ! "We love Him because He first loved us" means that we love with His love: by God's Holy Spirit. Dwell today on the loving nature of Jesus Christ in your life, and think of Him, as He has set it in his heart to love you unconditionally.

(read & chew)

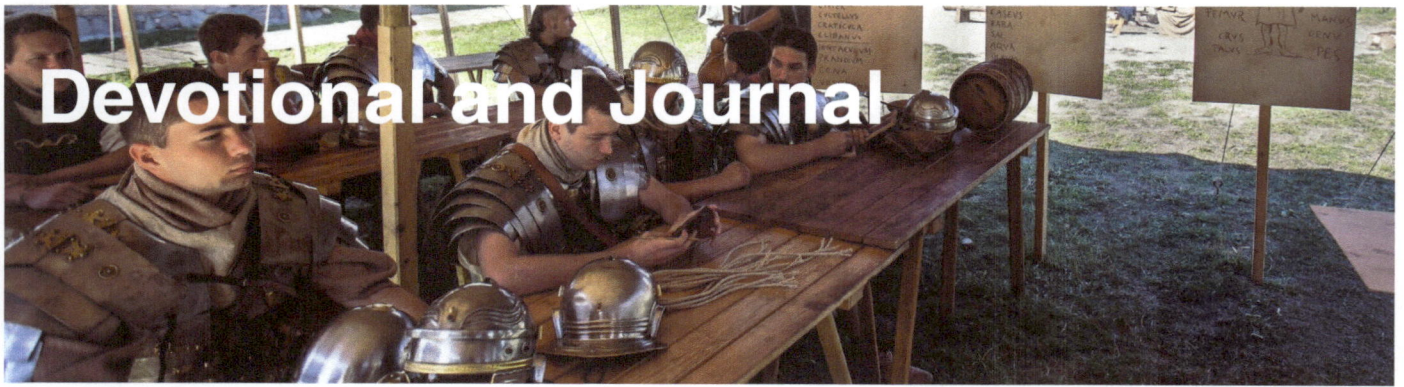

Devotional and Journal

Dear Gentlemen,

Take a quick moment to reflect on this:

1st John 3:1 says, "behold, what manner of love the Father has given unto us, that we should be called the sons of God..."

(read & chew)

What a privilege it is to belong to God, and to be his sons! Are you proud of your father? How much more, then, of your Heavenly Father? The love of God envelops us in the shadows of His wings. David teaches us that we are the apple of of His eye and are hidden in the shadows of His wings in Psalm 17:6-9.

> "I call on You, my God, for You will answer me;
> turn Your ear to me and hear my prayer.
> Show me the wonders of Your great love,
> You who save by Your right hand
> those who take refuge in You from their foes.
> Keep me as the apple of Your eye;
> hide me in the shadow of Your wings
> from the wicked who are out to destroy me,
> from my mortal enemies who surround me."

We rest in the security of His love and assurance. It is from here that we launch out to love others. As his son, take a moment and sing praises to Him! Thank him for His endless love that is a commitment of His will to you. Learn to bring this love into your own lives and will (determine in your heart) to love others as He has loved you.

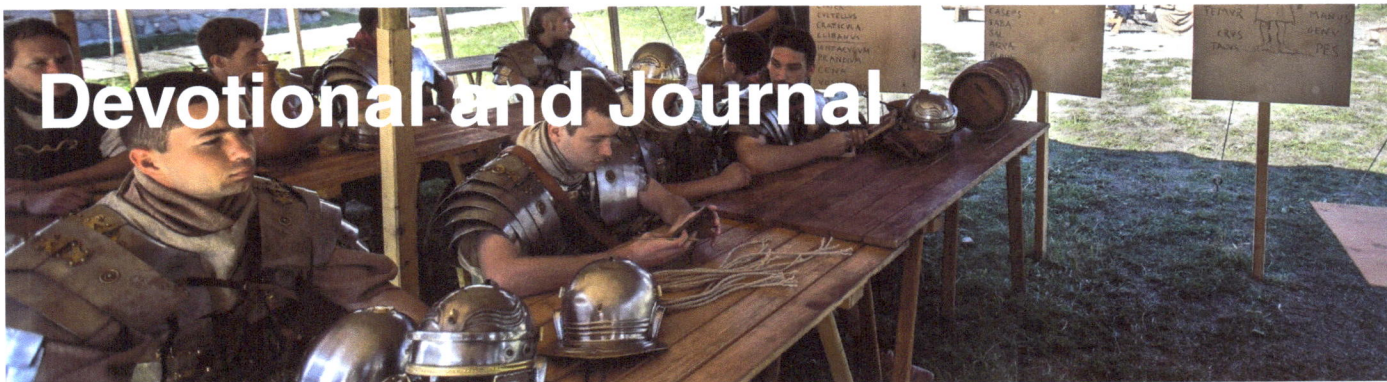

Devotional and Journal

Dear Gentlemen,

The love of God is the motivating factor of my life. Paul said it this way in

2nd Corinthians 5:13-16

"If we are 'out of our mind,' as some say, it is for God; if we are in our right mind, it is for you. For Christ's love compels us, because we are convinced that one died for all, and therefore all died. And He died for all, that those who live should no longer live for themselves but for Him who died for them and was raised again. So from now on we regard no one from a worldly point of view."

(read & chew)

One of the hardest experiences in life is to live with someone who once said they loved you, who no longer exhibits anything that remotely resembles love within the relationship. The hurt from those people's lives is a powerful force in all who know them. Imagine an apathetic partner who just does not care...

In Revelation 2:4-5, Jesus speaks of a church (a group of people gathered in His name) that has abandoned the love they had at first. They were busy, not quitters, but they were working without the love. Jesus tells them to return to their first love and to do the works they did at first.

"Yet I hold this against you: You have forsaken the love you had at first. Consider how far you have fallen! Repent and do the things you did at first. If you do not repent, I will come to you and remove your lamp stand from its place."

(read & chew)

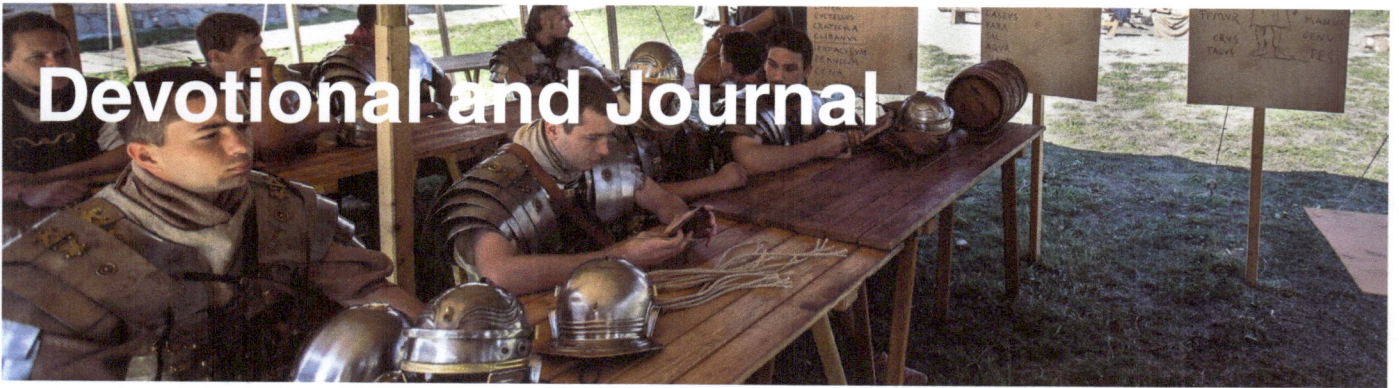

Devotional and Journal

Dear Gentlemen,

Yet I hold this against you: You have forsaken the love you had at first. Consider how far you have fallen! Repent and do the things you did at first. If you do not repent, I will come to you and remove your lamp stand from its place.

(read & chew)

The church in Revelation 2:4-5 had become doctrinaire and turned inward. Remember, the motivating factor in Christ is love. If we love God, then we will love what God loves, which is people; we will also work on what God's purpose for us is, which is to lead people into an eternal relationship with Him through Jesus Christ.

If you are having a problem loving others, then let me remind you of two possible issues you may be having:

1.) You cannot share what you do not have. In other words, you've never really surrendered to God, and His love is not in you.

OR

2.) You have God, but you have shut Him out of your life because of your bitterness towards the past. Your inability to forgive hinders your ability to love. Not loving someone is not an option.

(read & chew)

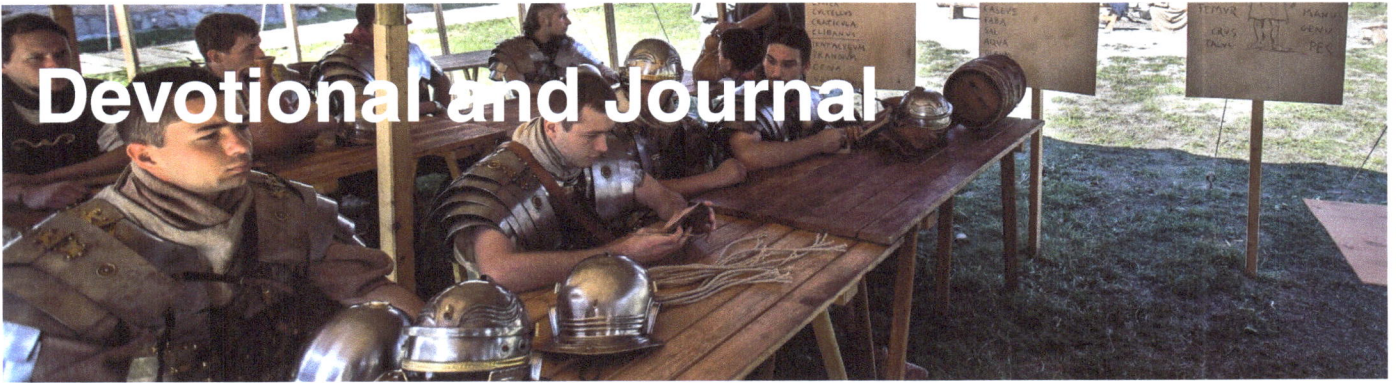

Devotional and Journal

Dear Gentlemen,

Your qualifications for all ministries are severely limited when you don't fully portray a loving deportment. Jesus' real love was quite tough on sinners in the area of their character flaws. Those flaws are the things that drive out the men who pretend to be righteous. Jesus was very hard on men who saw themselves as "having it all together;" men with superior ideas of themselves.

Jesus used strong, and oftentimes, hurtful words to crack the cold callous shell of pride that surrounded self-sufficient religious men. Hollywood and the Biblically illiterate world have created a politically correct, "sissified" Jesus who gushes feminine empathy to everyone at all times and under all circumstances. So this baits the question: What kind of love did Jesus portray? He portrayed the love of a father who is developing the character of his son...

"God's call to any man, and the anointing of the Spirit for service,
are conditioned upon that man's heart response."

- Alan Redpath

"The Spirit you received does not make you slaves, so that you live in fear again; rather, the Spirit you received brought about your adoption to sonship. And by Him we cry, 'Abba, Father.'"

(Abba is aramaic for "Daddy")

Romans 8:15

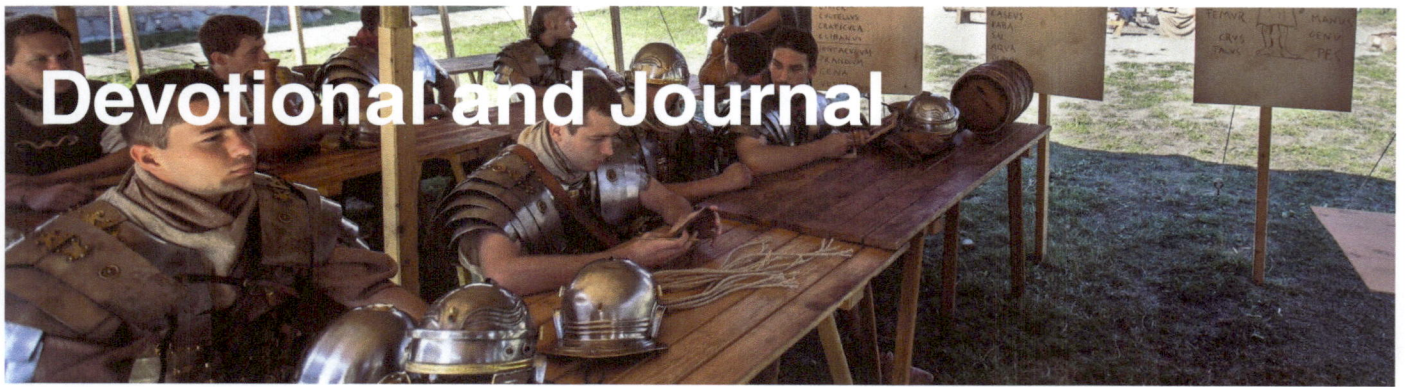

Devotional and Journal

Dear Gentlemen,

Let's talk about the agape love that Jesus exhibited. On the one hand, He was brutally tough on the pride and sin that we overlook when we are judging others. He gave no quarter and could preach and teach a crowd down from 5,000 to 12– because His "teachings were hard..."

John 6:60 – 66

On hearing it, many of His disciples said, "This is a hard teaching. Who can accept it?"Aware that His disciples were grumbling about this, Jesus said to them, "Does this offend you? Then what if you see the Son of Man ascend to where He was before! The Spirit gives life; the flesh counts for nothing. The words I have spoken to you—they are full of the Spirit and life. Yet there are some of you who do not believe." For Jesus had known from the beginning which of them did not believe and who would betray Him. He went on to say, "This is why I told you that no one can come to Me unless the Father has enabled them." From this time many of His disciples turned back and no longer followed Him.

(read & chew)

Basically, Jesus was one "tough-as-nails hombre," who on the one hand demanded absolute allegiance, yet on the other hand loved you so much that He would die for you. He could even die for people who did not like Him. He loved us so much that He would take our punishment and pay for all of it, even while no one—not one of us— believed in Him. In Ephesians 5, the apostle Paul intermingles a description of Christ's love for us with an illustration of how men are to reflect that love within their families. Read Ephesians 5:

Husbands, love your wives, just as Christ loved the church and gave Himself up for her to make her holy, cleansing her by the washing with water through the Word, and to present her to Himself as a radiant church, without stain or wrinkle or any other blemish, but holy and blameless. In this same way, husbands ought to love their wives as their own bodies. He who loves his wife loves himself. After all, no one ever hated his own body, but he feeds and cares for his body, just as Christ does the church, for we are members of His body. "For this reason a man will leave his father and mother and be united to his wife, and the two will become one flesh." This is a profound mystery—but I am talking about Christ and the church. However, each one of you also must love his wife as he loves himself, and the wife must respect her husband.

(read & chew)

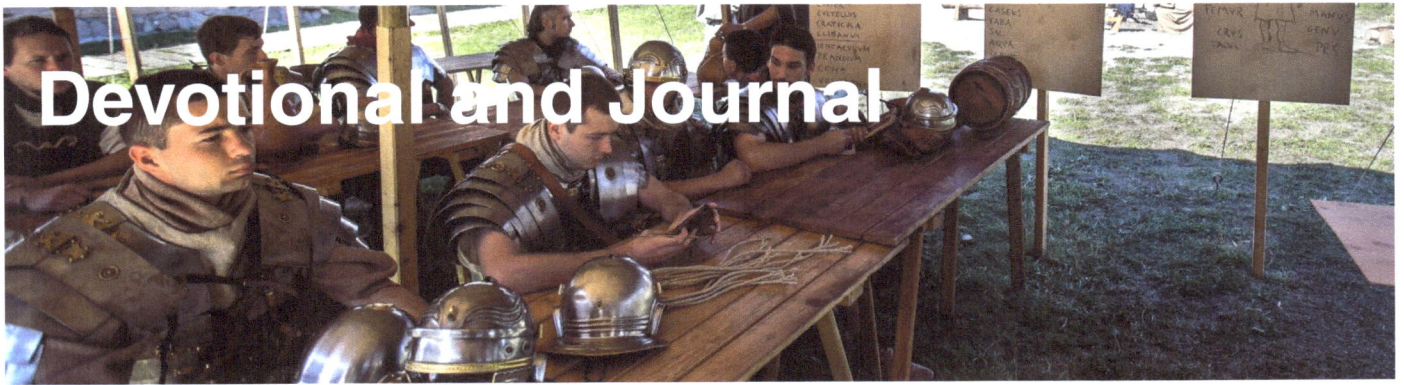

Devotional and Journal

Continued...

The love of "agape" is the love of covenant. It is an unconditional commitment kept by the strength of a transformed man's will. It is not based on feelings, but on a contract between you and your God; i.e., I will love my wife as You have loved me—without condition. Gentlemen, this is the love that rides out the emotional weaknesses of the woman. This love we learn from God, and we are also to practice it at home. Do this and you will become the "rock," the safe haven for your wife and you will be that—without demanding it—leader of your home.

(read & chew)

Devotional and Journal

Gentlemen,

God cannot be mocked; He is not some "pansy" that we can deceive. Jesus knows people's real motives. In Matthew 15:8, He says:

"These people honor me with their lips, but their hearts are far from me. They worship me in vain; their teachings are merely human rules."

(read & chew)

We are responsible to maintain a pure heart every day. God knows our heart, our innermost thoughts. Jeremiah 17:9 – 10, teaches us that "our hearts are deceitful and wicked above all things." Jeremiah then asked: "Who can understand it?"

(read & chew).

He then answered for God, "I the Lord search the heart and examine the mind..."

(read & chew)

Choice: You can either live in delusional denial or come to grips with the fact that God, the Creator of the world, knows your heart.

You then have to ask yourself the question: What in my heart needs to change today?

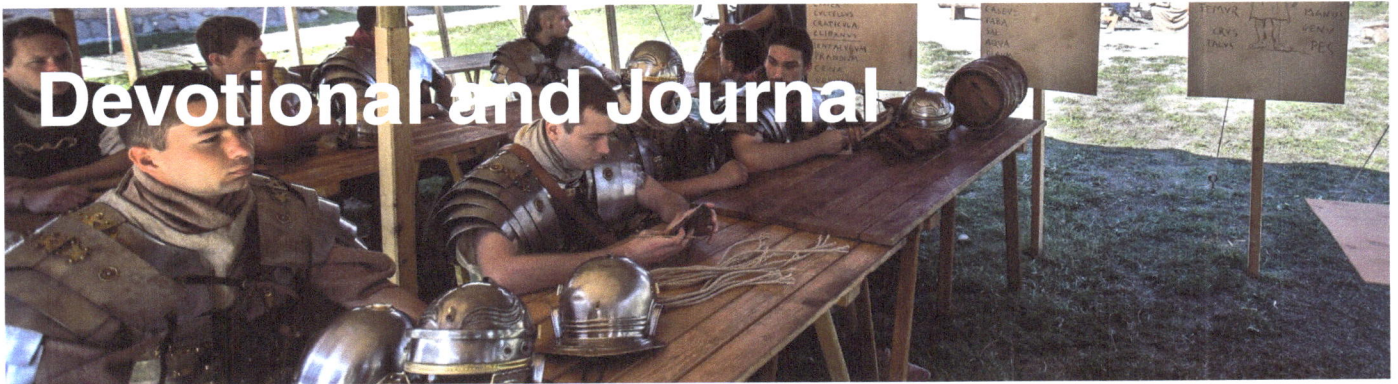

Devotional and Journal

Gentlemen,

I have stressed to you that the control of your mouth is one of the greatest masteries you can have. Jesus said in Matthew 15:18 that the "things that come out of a person's mouth come from the heart, and these defile them."

(read & chew)

If evil thoughts, murder, adultery, sexual immorality, theft, false testimony, and slander are regularly proceeding from your heart, using your mouth as a super-highway, you have a "Heart Issue." To control the heart, one must take a daily trip to the knees and to the Word. Taste and see what God has for you each day. I also find that staying away from the worldly stuff like movies and T.V. helps me to focus more on God. My falls into sin are usually small and incremental, but they can accumulate if I don't get time with God. I have found that I cannot spend time with God and not deal with the impurities of my heart.

> "Before we can pray, "Lord, Thy Kingdom come," we must be willing to pray, "My Kingdom go."
> - Alan Redpath

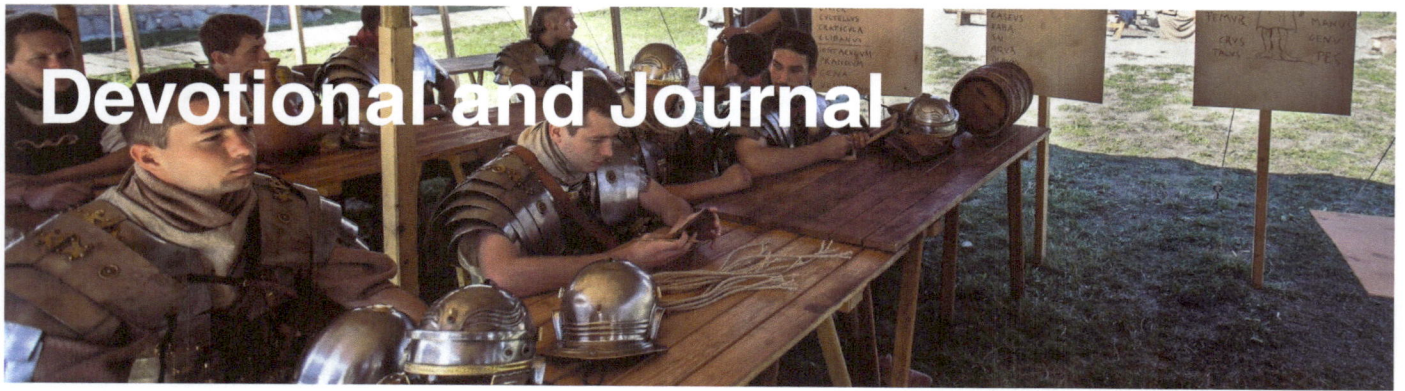

Dear Gentlemen,

This one thing I ask of you all: that each of you aspire to be a man after God's own heart! Paul said this concerning the rational for God's choice of David to be King, after removing Saul:

"God testified concerning him: I have found David son of Jesse,
a man after my own heart;
he will do everything that I want him to do."

Acts 13:22 & 1Samuel 3:14

(read & chew)

At this time, the sovereign God knew all that David would do, both good and bad. God chose David because he would be a doer of the Word and not a hearer only. How did David become this man with "a heart that God loves?" First, David believed in his God and bragged about Him. Place this in your heart as you say it: "Who are you to stand against the Army of the living God?" There is no one like my God! There is no one like my Daddy! All good Dads love their Sons!

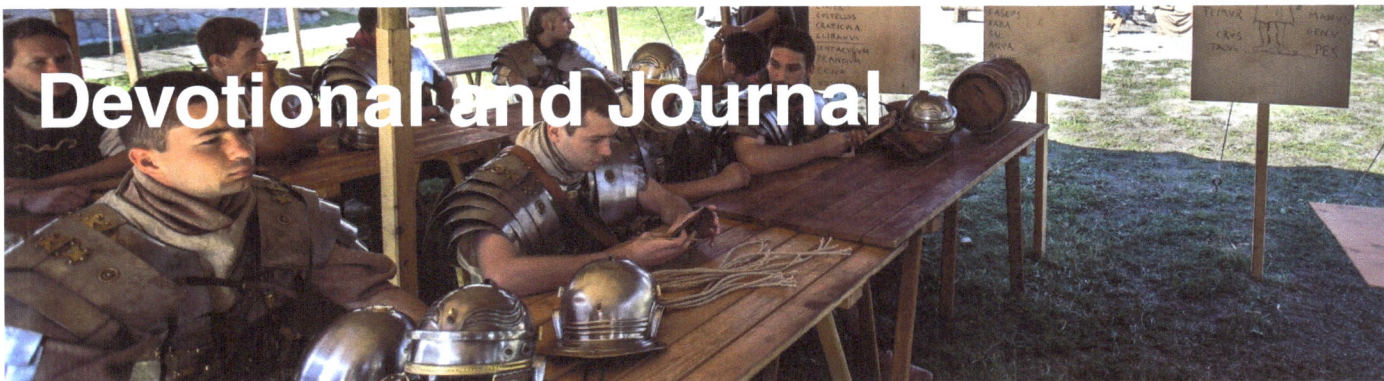

Devotional and Journal

Dear Gentlemen,

The second character trait of David's heart was that he was willing to stand against God's foes even if it meant standing alone.

1 Samuel 17 (look up, and read & chew)

As a young man, he lived by the principle that I have tried to teach you: In my heart, I have determined to choose ahead of time to do the right thing, by God, no matter what. I will not poll other men and their opinions to determine right from wrong. I will set my heart to follow God and His Word.

Even though you may feel and find yourself standing alone against some giants, I can assure you that you are certainly being watched by the world! When the giant Goliath fell, those watching gained heart. Even though it seems the world wants you to fail, I believe that they truly are looking for giant killers...God save us!

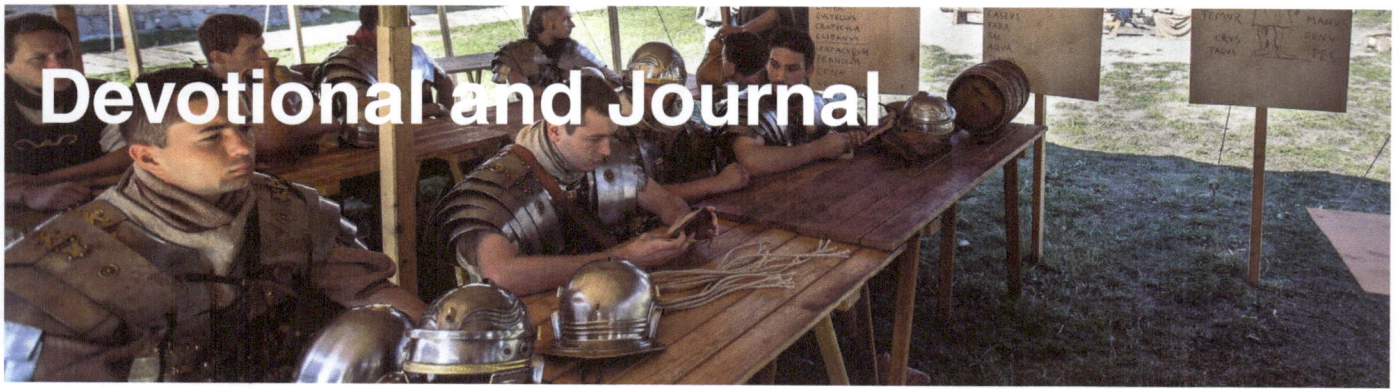

Dear Gentlemen,

1 Samuel 17 (re-read & re-chew)

David, for all of his shortcomings, was a man who knew how to repent. He trusted God like a boy learning to ride a new bike with his dad. The boy knew that, even if he messed up and fell, his father would never abandon him. David always understood that God was not after his perfection, but was after David's relationship of loyalty. Loyalty to God is a man's greatest character trait. The Disciples learned this in the Garden of Gethsemane. They were utter failures at the trial and crucifixion, and even after the resurrection—they still wanted worldly authority and power up. It wasn't until Jesus ascended and the Holy Spirit entered their lives that they finally "got it." In between the mountain of ascension and the outpouring of the Holy Spirit at Pentecost, they had to learn to pray and helplessly wait on God. Not one of them would ever betray Him again.

Loyalty till death...

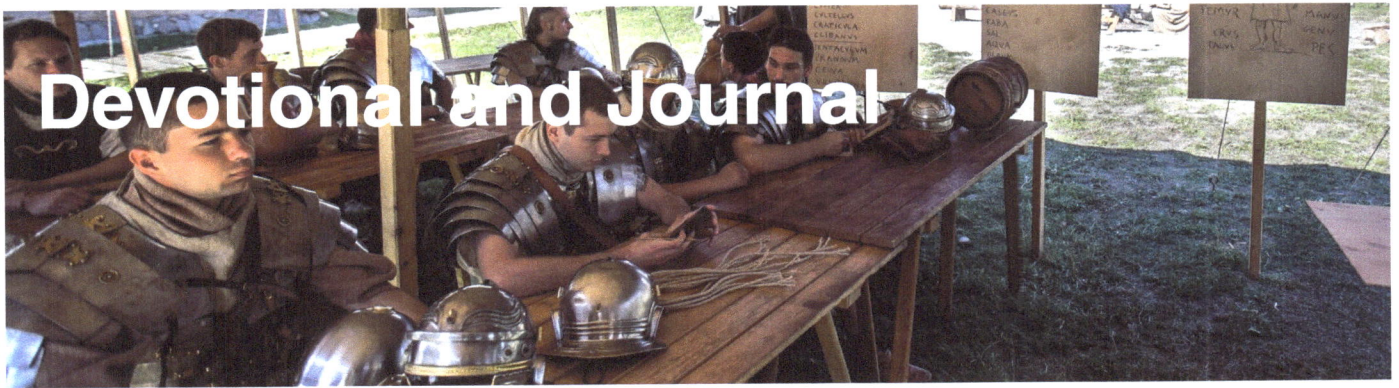

Devotional and Journal

Dear Gentlemen,

2nd Samuel 24:24

"But the king replied to Araunah, "No, I insist on paying you for it. I will not sacrifice to the Lord my God burnt offerings that cost me nothing."

and 1 Samuel 17 (David & Goliath)

(read & chew)

At the end of David's life, he sinned greatly by numbering his troops in order to calculate his battle worthiness. God was insulted because David had always fought by faith with God's intervention, not with man's plans. So God punished David and his people. David recognized his sin quickly, repented and prepared to offer sacrifice for his sin.

A local man offered to give him land for the altar and animals for the sacrifice. David said to the man a profound truth: "I will not offer to God that which cost me nothing." So he bought the land and the sacrifice with his own money.

Never offer to God that which cost you nothing. If your tithe does not cause you to trust in God for your finances, then increase it until you trust! Do not offer God what is easy for you, but trust God and fully rely on Him to meet every need.

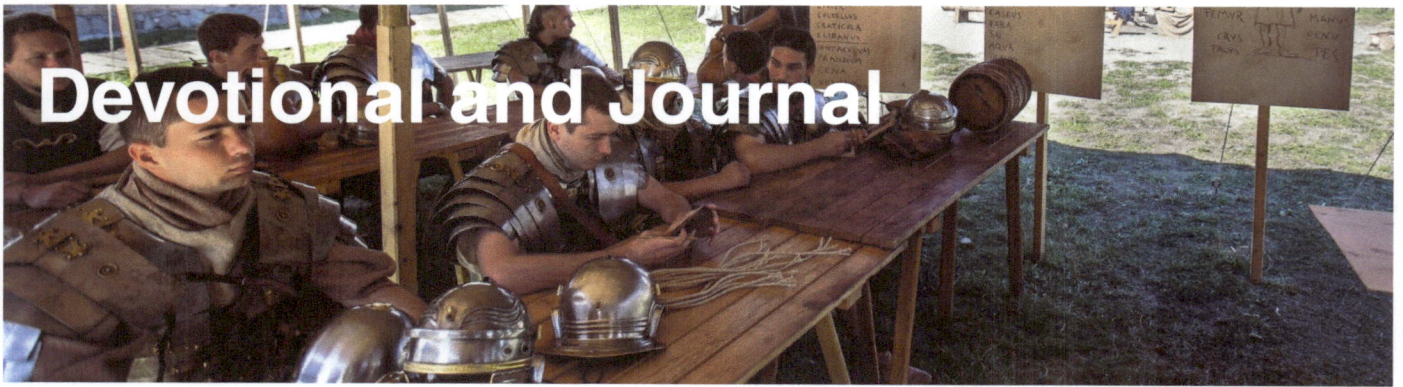

Dear Gentlemen,

David knew himself, and he knew that if his heart was not clean, he could not be in right relationship with God. He treasured his time with God. He knew how to approach the throne of God and was a "type" of the Christian who was yet to come: one who could boldly enter the throne room of God.

Hebrews 4:16

"Let us then approach God's throne of grace with confidence, so that we may receive mercy and find grace to help us in our time of need."

(read & chew)

In Psalm 51:10, David prayed:

"Create in me a clean heart, oh God, and renew a right spirit within me."

(read & chew)

I urge you, by the mercies of God, to never approach a major decision of life without making a safety check on the purity of your heart.

Ask God to cleanse you...He loves you too!

Hold on to Jesus, boys!

P.S. Keeping the heart clean is the daily procedure of dying to self; brush your teeth, wash your face...and cleanse your heart!

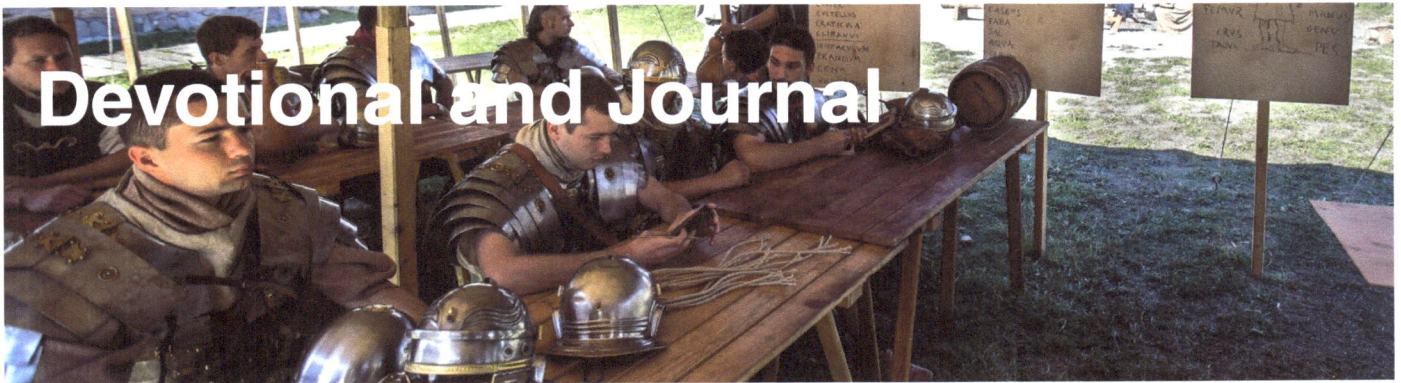

Devotional and Journal

Gentlemen,

As a little boy, I looked up to my Grandfathers more than any other men. They were "giants" to me, who carried me on their shoulders so high that I could touch the ceilings. Grandfather Christie was a great Baptist pastor in Northern Virginia. He helped start the First Baptist Church of Woodbridge, and then pastored Bon Air Baptist Church of Arlington. What was obvious about his life was the fact that he loved God.

In the summers of my childhood we would visit him in Arlington. I used to love to sleep in grand-dad's room. Before he slept, we would pray. He would kneel on the floor with his hands folded together beside the bed. There he poured out his heart for all of us before God. It would take me years to learn how important it was to kneel down. I find God when I'm on my face, down on the floor. Bow, therefore, and learn to know in whose presence you dare to enter! Bow before the King of Kings; your Lord.

Psalm 95: 1-7

"Come, let us sing for joy to the Lord; let us shout aloud to the Rock of our salvation. Let us come before Him with thanksgiving and extol Him with music and song. For the Lord is the great God, the great King above all gods. In His hand are the depths of the earth, and the mountain peaks belong to Him. The sea is His, for He made it, and His hands formed the dry land. Come, let us bow down in worship, let us kneel before the Lord our Maker; for He is our God and we are the people of His pasture, the flock under His care."

(read & chew)

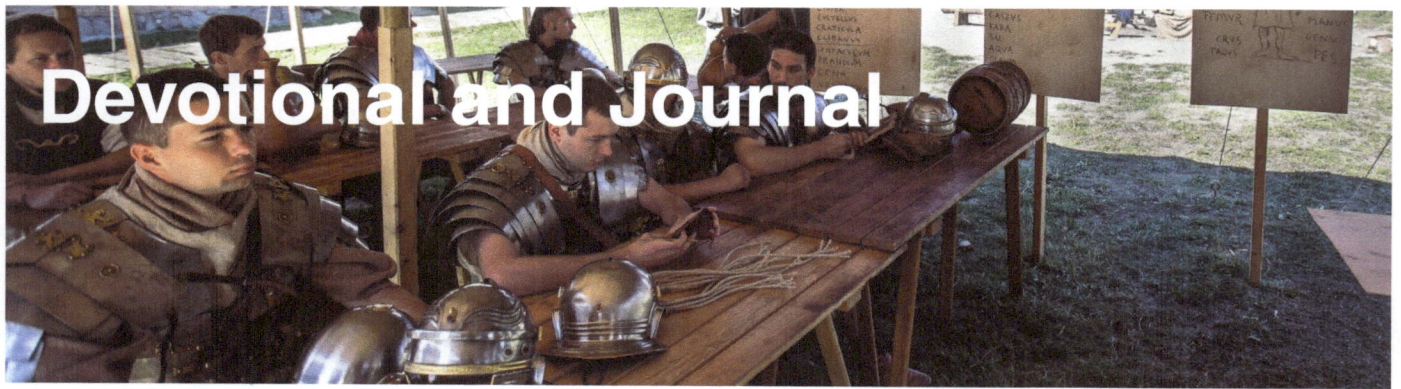

Devotional and Journal

Gentlemen,

There is a tendency today to be "too familiar" with the Holy things of God. God forbid that we should be even remotely casual about the glory of being in God's presence, especially after Jesus having saved us and now being at the right hand of the Father. After we have checked the conditions of our hearts, Paul tells us in Hebrews 10:19 that we...

"...have confidence to enter the most holy place by the blood of Jesus, by a new and living way open for us through the curtain, that is, His body."

(read & chew)

Be aware that there is a decorum mentioned, a protocol for our behavior in the presence of royalty. Before we enter the presence of the King, our hearts must be sprinkled by Christ's blood and washed with pure water. It is only Jesus who can do this amazing thing for us. No one enters the presence of the King without the wedding garment provided by the Father!

In Matthew 22:12, Jesus says:

"and he said to him, 'Friend, how did you come in here without wedding clothes?' And the man was speechless."

"Praise God, from whom all blessings flow;
Praise Him, all creatures here below;
Praise Him above, ye heav'nly host;
Praise Father, Son, and Holy Ghost."

(read & chew Mt. 22 about the wedding banquet)

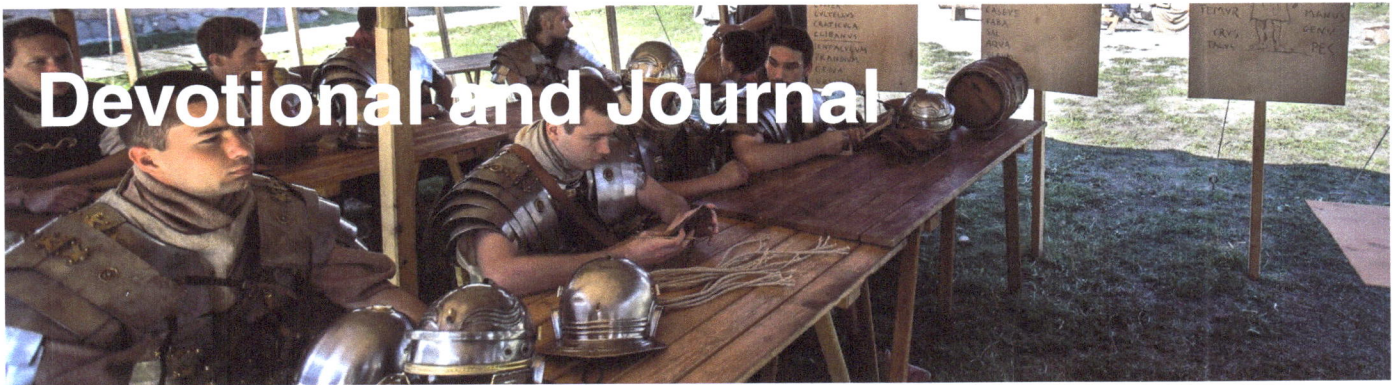

Devotional and Journal

Dear Gentlemen,

As the world becomes less and less under the "Christian influence," note that the Scriptures tell us in Matthew 24:12, that in the last days the hearts of men will grow cold. This is in reference to the Gospel of Jesus Christ and God.

Let me share my heart with you: worship is going to be challenged. No matter what, never bow down to, nor even tacitly acknowledge another god. As believers in Christ, our progenitors suffered from death at the hands of lions; they were burned alive as human torches; dipped alive in wax, and then impaled upon sticks lining Nero's personal path to the Colosseum. Deuteronomy 4:23-24 tells us to...

"...be careful not to forget the covenant of the Lord your God that He made with you: do not make for yourselves an idol in the form of anything the Lord your God has forbid, for the Lord your God is a consuming fire, a jealous God."

(read & chew)

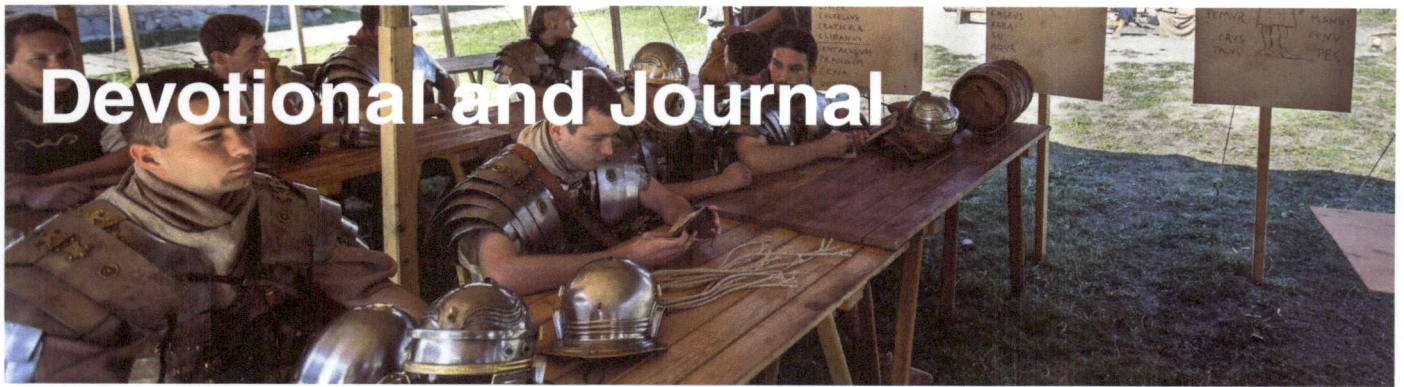

Contimued...

You will be tempted by the world to participate in "moments of silence," which are in design, purposed to silence Christians. Pray out loud anyway; seek not to offend men with your brashness, but seek not to offend God with your participation in such anti-God and atheistic farces.

We MUST NOT BE SILENCED!

Say the Lord's prayer quietly and respectfully. This prayer is the model prayer of Jesus and is offensive only to the atheist. Either way, an atheist has no right to block your freedom of speech and expression. Ponder on this: They are demanding you not to talk to someone they think does not exist.

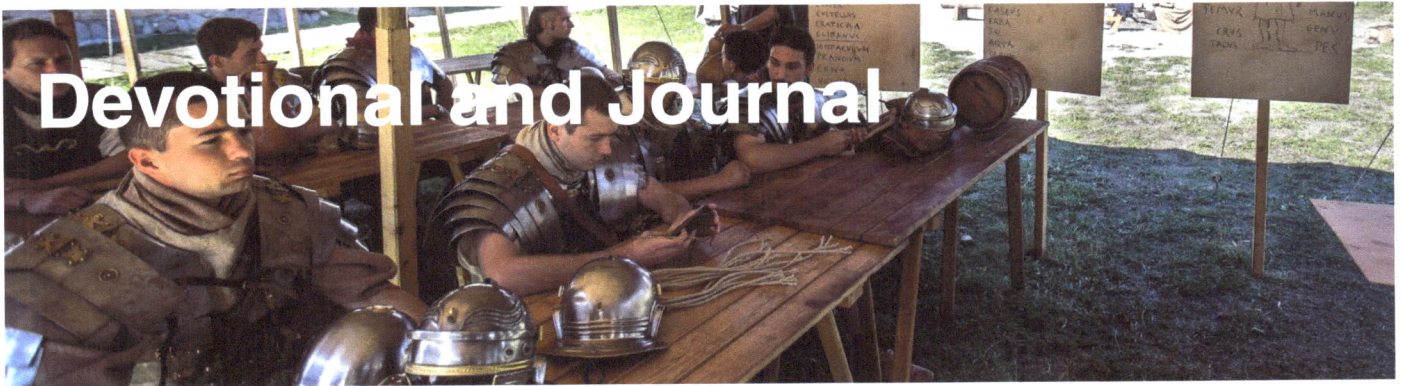

Devotional and Journal

Dear Gentlemen,

Music in itself is neither Christian nor non-Christian. It's the words that make a difference. Although, I don't care for certain types of sounds, I understand God can be worshiped in many different genres. I think there are two important aspects to recognize: whatever is done should be done to glorify Christ and serve to prepare the heart to receive the Word of God.

Music can set the emotional tone for the service by opening our hearts to hear God speak. Men, we lead our families in the worship part of the service.

1st Timothy 2:8 says:

"therefore I want the men everywhere to pray, lifting up holy hands without anger or disputing."

(read & chew)

You, as men, set the worship for the whole body of Christ. Take it upon yourselves to lead your family and your church in the praise of God!

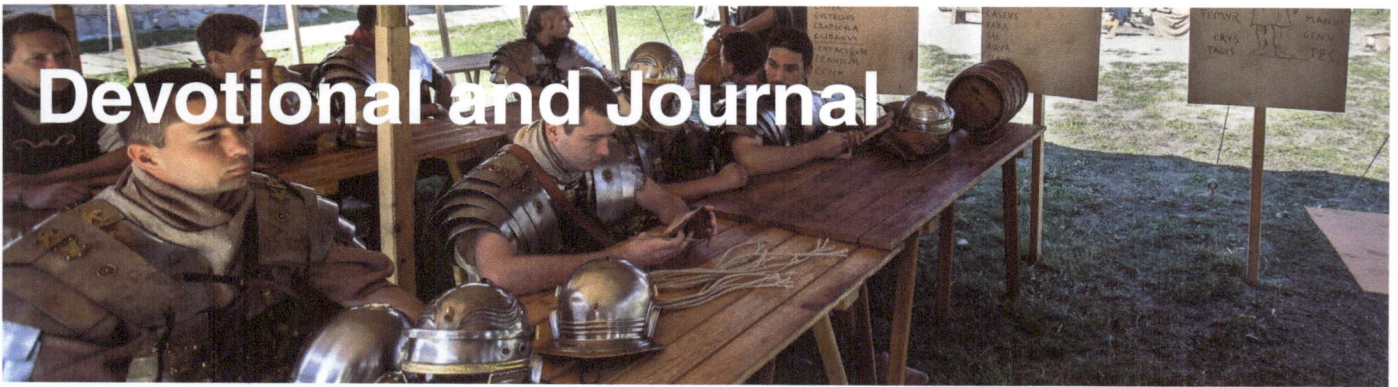

Devotional and Journal

Dear Gentlemen,

Let's talk about prayer in the worship time. Jesus does not want us to pray for show, but to focus on Him. This is why He recommended praying under the prayer shawl, to the men of His time.

Matthew 6:6

"But when you pray, go into your room, close the door and pray to your Father, who is unseen. Then your Father, who sees what is done in secret, will reward you."

(read & chew)

Today's modern services have missed the power of prayer. Many of our men and women pray in vain repetition using a cliché prayer language loaded with excessively repetitious verbiage. The nervous chatter of "Father God, Father God, Father God, mingled between every other phrase in the prayer life, is just one example. Watch for "catch phrases" of words that are used just to fill space within a sentence (a modern favorite is "Lord, be with us, or with so and so." Really? Like He is not?). If you were to talk to your friends like that, repeating their name every other phrase, they will think that you are nuts or crazy. Prayer is a holy conversation with God. Slow down the meaningless verbiage, and let every word of your mouth and every thought of your heart be blended into reverent and well-thought-out, meaningful sentences!

P.S. There is no such thing as a "silent" prayer in Scriptures.

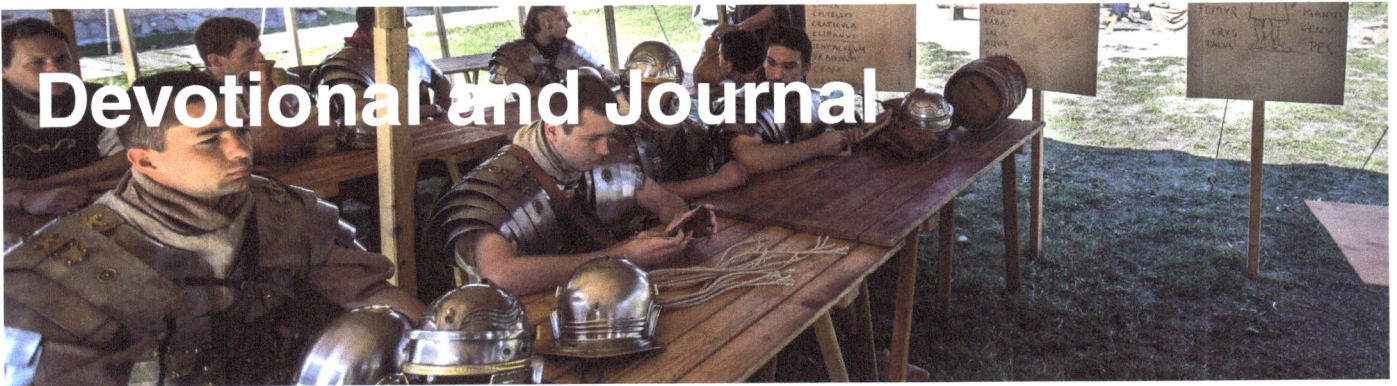

Devotional and Journal

Dear Gentlemen,

Do your best to take Sunday off and make worship a priority, first for yourself, but also for the family. The fact that you are not working on the Lord's Day, honoring His desire, is of greater value to you and to God than you can imagine.

Hebrews 4: 8–11

"For if Joshua had given them rest, God would not have spoken later about another day. There remains, then, a Sabbath-rest for the people of God; for anyone who enters God's rest also rests from their works, just as God did from His. Let us, therefore, make every effort to enter that rest, so that no one will perish by following their example of disobedience."

(read & chew)

This passage teaches us that by believing in Jesus Christ, we enter into the Sabbath rest of salvation. Verse 16, in the same chapter, tells us that this work of Jesus Christ enables us to enter God's throne of grace with confidence:

"Let us then approach God's throne of grace with confidence, so that we may receive mercy and find grace to help us in our time of need."

Man was not made to work seven days a week. We need to set a day of focus aside, once a week, to meet with the Ekklessia (Greek for church) for the purposes of God. Make an intentional effort to take the bulk of your time on Sundays to worship God. Find that quiet place of solitude sometime during the day, where you can focus in prayer and Bible study, while you seek the will of God for your family and your life.

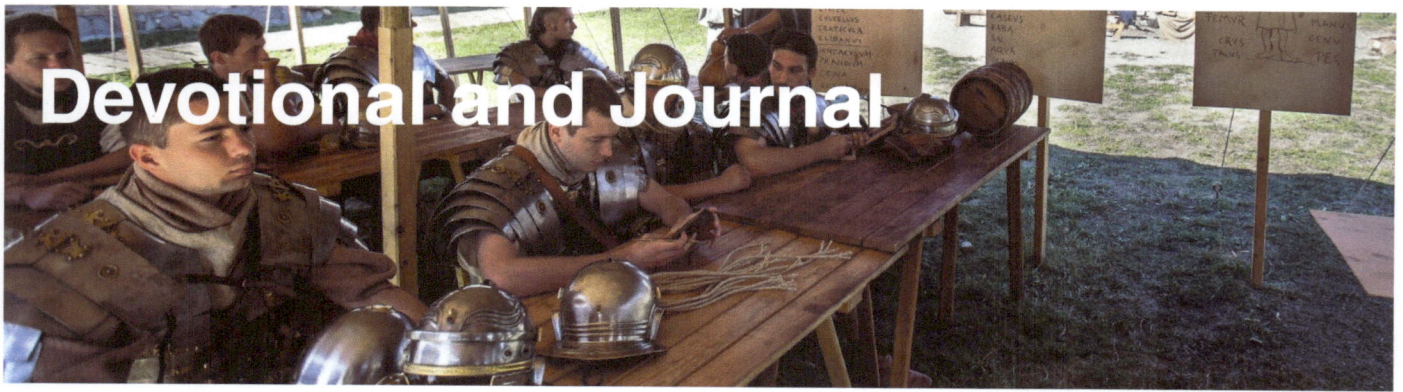

Week 8 / Day 7

Dear Gentlemen,

One of my favorite verses calls us to come together and worship— and to make it a habit.

Hebrews 10:25 teaches us that:

"...we are not to forsake meeting together, as some are in the habit of doing."

(read & chew)

Worship is done corporately. When the whole body of Christ unites in purpose and worships God, you can sense the presence of God in the place of meeting.

Some people feel that they can worship anywhere. While this is true of individual worship, it is limited. Frankly, worship is a group or corporate experience. King David said in

Psalm 96:6

"O come let us worship and bow down: let us kneel before the Lord our God and maker, for He is our God and we are the people of His pasture and the sheep of His hand."

(read & chew)

Today, will you hear His voice?

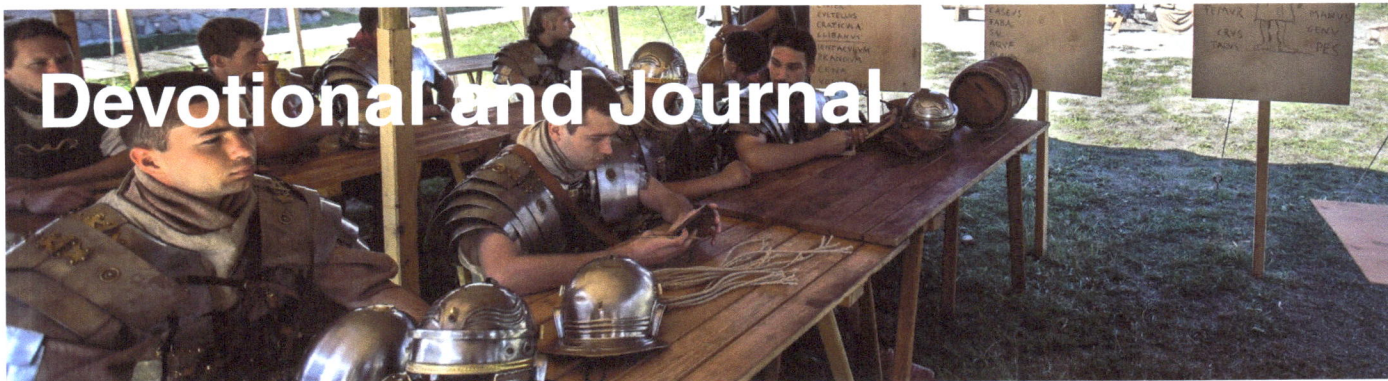

Devotional and Journal

Gentlemen,

Today I am your armor bearer. I'm here to outfit you with the latest technological arms for you to be able to fight in an intergalactic war that stretches from the height of heaven to the region of earth and then to the pit of hell. We do not, gentlemen, wage this war as the world does, but with spiritual armor that will tear down strongholds and defeat the gates of hell.

(read & chew Ephesians 6:10-18 for this week)

"Finally, be strong in the Lord and in his mighty power. Put on the full armor of God, so that you can take your stand against the devil's schemes. For our struggle is not against flesh and blood, but against the rulers, against the authorities, against the powers of this dark world and against the spiritual forces of evil in the heavenly realms. Therefore put on the full armor of God, so that when the day of evil comes, you may be able to stand your ground, and after you have done everything, to stand. Stand firm then, with the belt of truth buckled around your waist, with the breastplate of righteousness in place, and with your feet fitted with the readiness that comes from the gospel of peace. In addition to all this, take up the shield of faith, with which you can extinguish all the flaming arrows of the evil one. Take the helmet of salvation and the sword of the Spirit, which is the word of God. And pray in the Spirit on all occasions with all kinds of prayers and requests. With this in mind, be alert and always keep on praying for all the Lord's people."

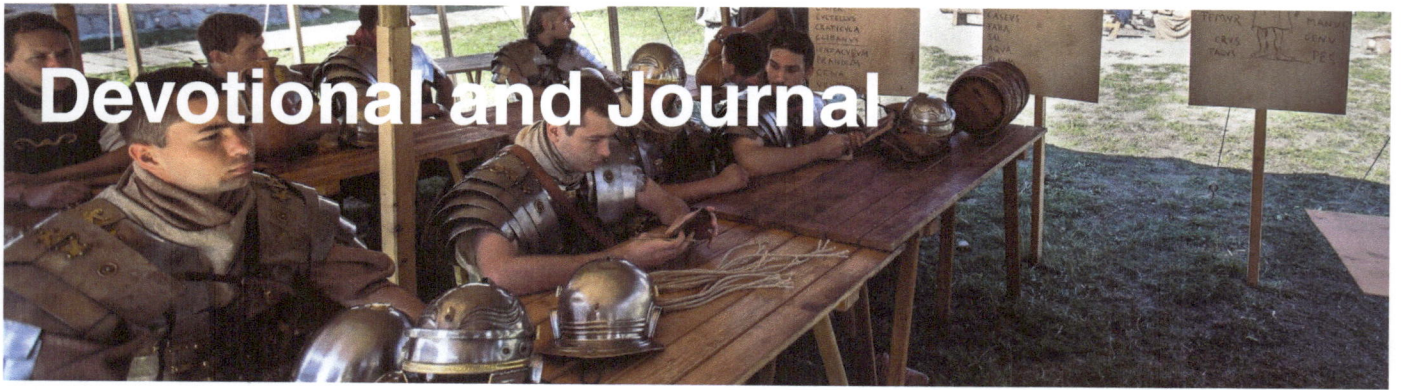

Continued...

Your orders, should you decide to accept them, are to join with your fellow soldiers and to stand firm. First, you will need to fasten on to yourself the belt of Truth around your waist. Why did Paul mention this first? Because in the Roman armor, the belt had two functions: First, it held all the other armor in place. On the belt, there was a hanger for the heavy shield, a latch to support the spear, a holder for the sword, and 6 to 8 grieves in the hanging in the front for protection of the groin area, which would absorb the impact of a low blow. Paul calls this the belt of Truth. We know that it is the living Truth of God's Word, the logos Factor. Essentially, the Word of God, absorbed and learned, holds all the armor parts into an integrated weapon system. None of the other pieces work without the living Word. Put the Word of God on today and every day. This is your intentional morning quiet time! Spend time today in the Living Word of God.

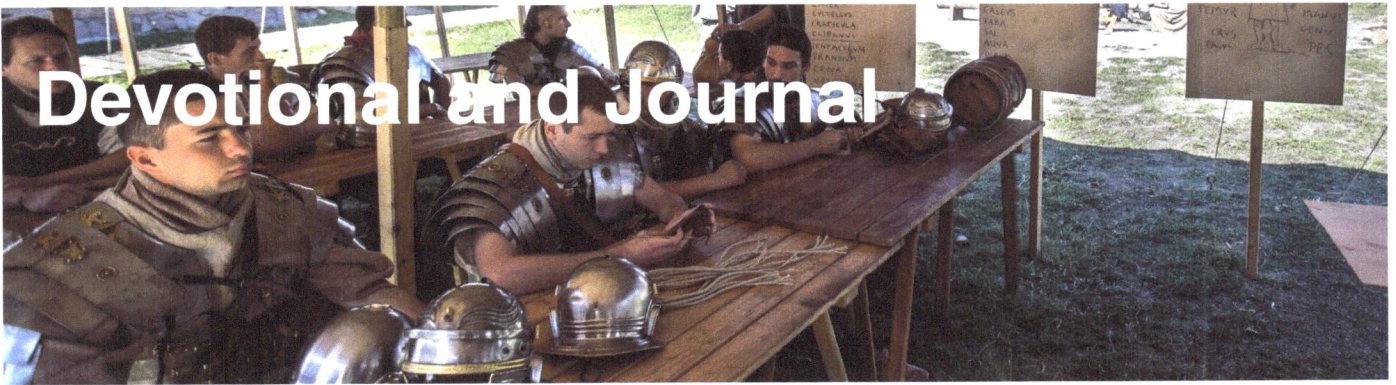

Devotional and Journal

Gentlemen,

(read & chew Ephesians 6:10-18; see page 14 for this week)

The breastplate of righteousness is the protector of your heart, and we call this the Kardia Factor. Every morning, check your heart and say: "create in me a clean heart, O lord." Otherwise, Satan will attack your heart and make you either feel like a hypocrite and silence you, or he will get your heart to grow foul and will get you to disqualify yourself for your ministry.

The Roman breastplate at the height of the Empire encompassed the whole chest with metal on the front and back. In fact, the Empire was not defeated in battle until the pressures of the complaints of the soldiers about the weight and discomfort of the breastplate were yielded to by the armor bearers. The breastplates were replaced with leather and the metal helmets were replaced with leather. The robust training necessary to carry the armor was reduced. Many historians attribute the collapse of the Roman legions in battle to these factors. Who said that warfare was easy or convenient? To succeed in warfare the men are drilled daily, both in the development of their physical stamina, and their proficiency with the weapons.

"When we confess our sin, God is faithful and just and will cleanse us and forgive our sin."

(read & chew 1st John 1:9)

How? By placing them onto Jesus who, in turn, gives us His righteousness. His armor for you is custom fit for your needs to protect your heart. He did His part on the Cross for you, so you must do your part with a purified heart ready for action for Him!

"The best place any Christian can ever be in is to be totally destitute
and totally dependent upon God, and know it."

- Alan Redpath

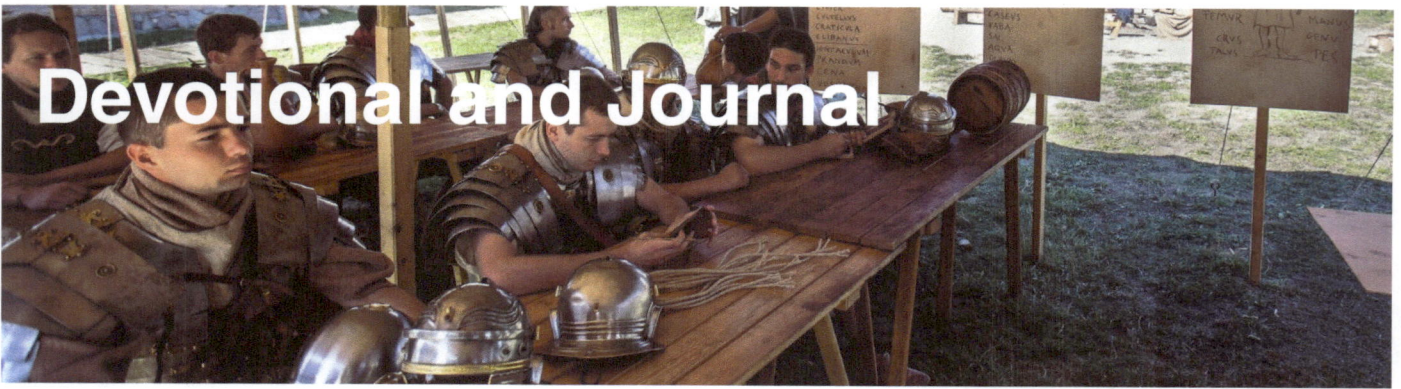

Devotional and Journal

Dear Gentlemen,

(Are you in or out? Seriously, are you going to go to battle for God? If so, you are going to need your feet to be wearing what I call "Nike" gospel shoes. The slogan for Nike shoes is _____ (fill in the blank).

The sandal of the Roman soldier had nail spikes coming out of the leather on the bottom of the feet, so as to give the soldier traction while standing in the *testugo* square formation. When Paul talks about standing, he is referring to how the soldiers could take on a full frontal attack of the enemy by foot, by horse, or by chariot. The *testugo* would not shake or move because the men dug in their feet together, linked arms together, and linked their shields together with their spears sticking out, forming a solid square mass of muscle that could not be broken.

When you preach the Good News of Jesus Christ, you are to shod your feet with the preparation of the Gospel of Christ. It is a Gospel that breaks the back of the enemy. Another word for the Gospel is Good News. It is the Gospel that pours smothering water onto the flames of hell! The Good News is simple and profound: 1) it starts with God's love... "God so loved the world" 2) Next, our sin and consequential judgment is paid for with God's gift... "He gave His only Son" to die on a Cross. 3) Then, if anyone desires to respond to God's love by believing in Jesus... "whosoever believes in Him." 4) That person will not have to die in their sin, but will be in heaven with God forever!

That's Good News!

(Scripture in red is from John 3:16; put to memory)

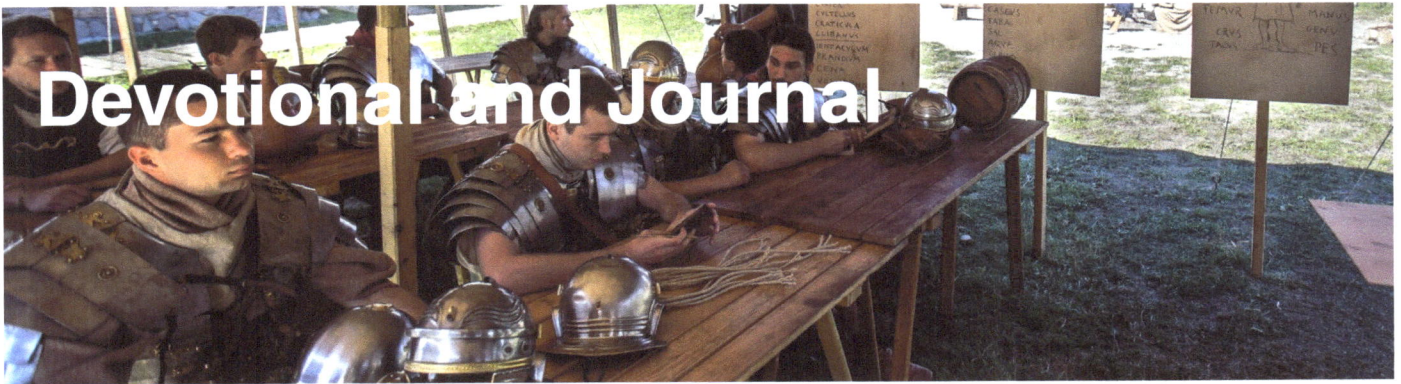

Devotional and Journal

Dear Gentlemen,

If the shield of faith is part of the daily armor of God that we are to wear, let us think about the function of the Roman Shield in battle. The Roman soldier shield was a large curved rectangle with an interlocking lip on the edge. In battle, the shields would be linked together with the others from the unit, forming what is called a testudo, and could withstand an aerial bombardment of arrows and rocks. It could even stop a direct charge of the chariot. In many ways, it was one of the most important parts of the Roman armor.

Your shield was more important for fighting in the unit than your sword or spear, because your comrades could replenish these items, but not your shield. As a result, when your shield was down, not only were you exposed to the darts of the enemy, but the men who were fighting to your left and to your right were exposed as well. It is important that you hold up your faith, which is your shield. The brothers that are around you can help you hold up your shield as well. I am talking about your faith in your walk with Christ.

Never let Satan attack your faith. If you need more faith, ask for help from God and your brothers. Should your shield fall, pull into the ranks of the men and regain your strength. There will be times when we will take our turn leading in faith, and there will be times when we need the covering of another. Know this: fight as a unit and you will always win! I've got your back!

"Faith, hope, and love...These three will remain."

1 Corinthians 13

(read & chew the chapter)

Continued...

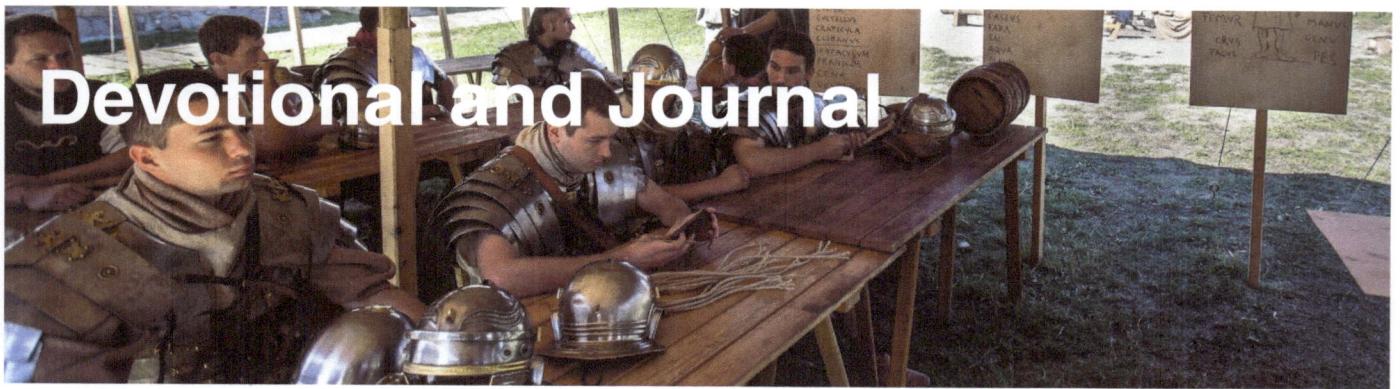

Continued...

What can you take to heaven with you? Faith, hope, and love. These three words define our character before God. The great men of the world all had human flaws. In Abraham's fear, he attempted to sell off his wife. Jacob deceived his father and brother. Moses killed a man, and David committed adultery. These imperfect men were not justified by their works, rather they each were justified by their faith in God's promise. They never surrendered hope in God and they loved God and respected the fact that He was, and is indeed, God. The men of God will fill up on faith, lean on God and his fellow men, and will never give up on His mission!

"Circumstances which we have resented, situations which we have found desperately difficult, have all been the means in the hands of God of driving the nails into the self-life which so easily complains."

- Alan Redpath

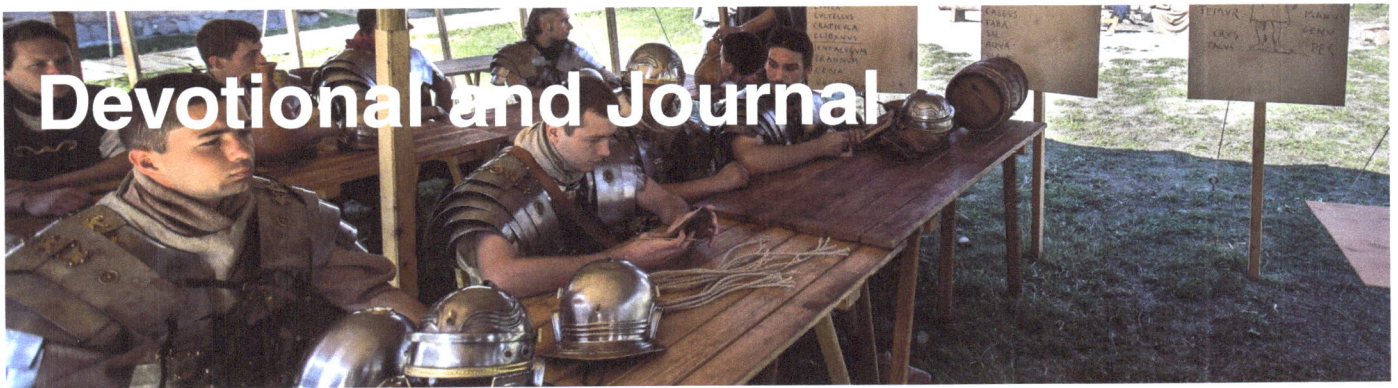

Devotional and Journal

Dear Gentlemen,

Today, we are introducing you to the latest technology in battle helmets. The Roman helmet was designed for high visibility with maximum and flexible security for the foot-soldier. The helmet had a large flange on the back similar to a modern fire helmet. Rocks and fire were common warfare tactics of that day, and this large flange protected the back of the neck down to the edge of the breastplate. Two loose-hinged metal flaps came off each side of the helmet, protecting the sides of the face while allowing an open center face that served the soldier for more precise communication and easier breathing during the battle.

The main purpose of the helmet and what it protects is obvious. It protects the brain. Paul's helmet of Salvation protects the mind in the area of security of our salvation. When you are experiencing doubts, nine times out of ten, you have not gone to battle with your helmet on. Religious debates have driven eternal security away from its purpose into the realm of arguments on free will. The concepts of absolute free will are imposed onto the Bible, and don't hold exegetical water. The concept of slavery to sin, on the one side, and that there are no choices regarding salvation on the other, are both lacking in systematic theological standing. Your security is not a matter of your will as to obtaining or losing salvation, nor is security about the overwhelming election of a sovereign God; rather, security is about ownership.

Continued...

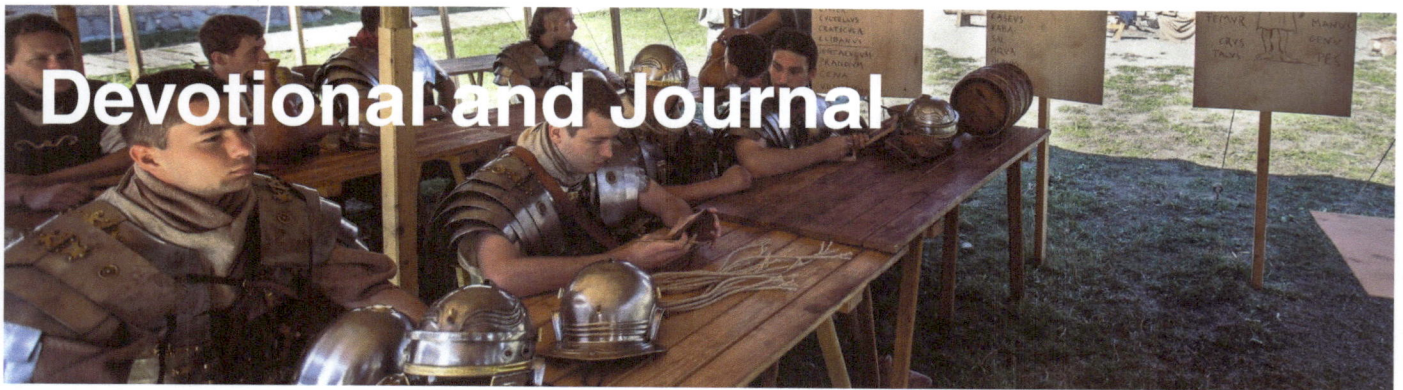

Continued

You have been purchased by God, and paid for with the deposit of the Holy Spirit into your life. We are neither capable to earn our salvation (which was accomplished and finished for us on the Cross), nor are we able, by our own free will, to cast off our salvation by choice, because our lives are not ours to cast off. Jesus owns our title; we can't sell ourselves off because we don't own our lives—He does.

So why does God do this? Because when you're in the battle for souls, God doesn't want you wondering if you are, or will remain saved. That account is paid for... tetelestai. The helmet is simple: it protects your thought life from doubts and evil penetration by the enemy. It is equipped with a Holy Spirit earpiece that sings into your soul when you attempt to sin. He is your early warning device. Listen to Him and adjust your targets!

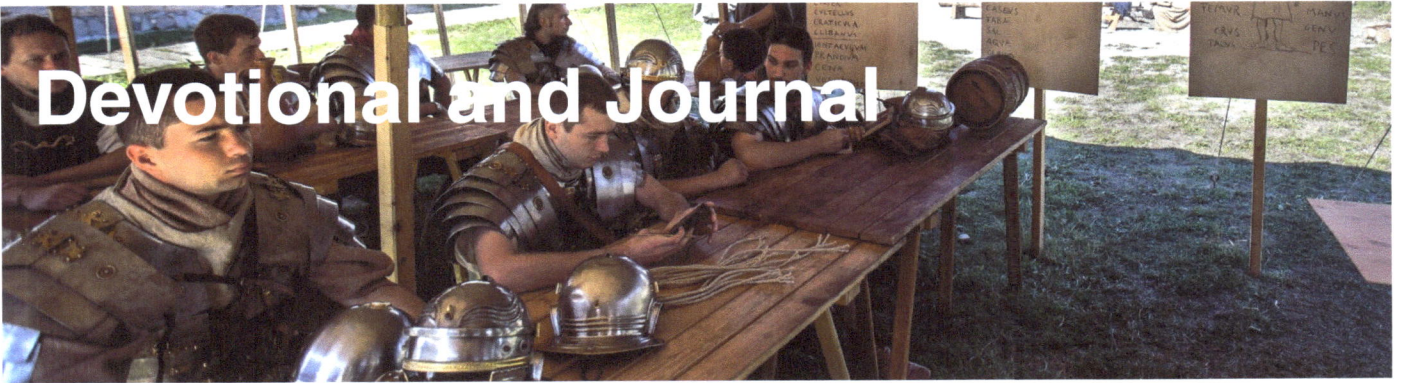

Devotional and Journal

Dear Gentlemen,

I present to you your sword. It is a technological wonder. This weapon has 66 featured weapons systems known as books. It has instructions from 40 intelligence specialists intent on your success. (There are 66 books in the Bible written by over 40 authors). The sword is an integrated fighting system with a supernatural digital system controlled from outside our time space continuum!

I introduce to you the inerrant, infallible, and proven-over thousands-of-years Word of the living God. This double edged blade stays eternally sharp and comes with a complete eternal guarantee. It will slice and dice any argument that comes against the knowledge of God.

(Meditate on this: Hebrews 4:12)

"For the word of God is alive and active. Sharper than any double-edged sword, it penetrates even to dividing soul and spirit, joints and marrow; it judges the thoughts and attitudes of the heart."

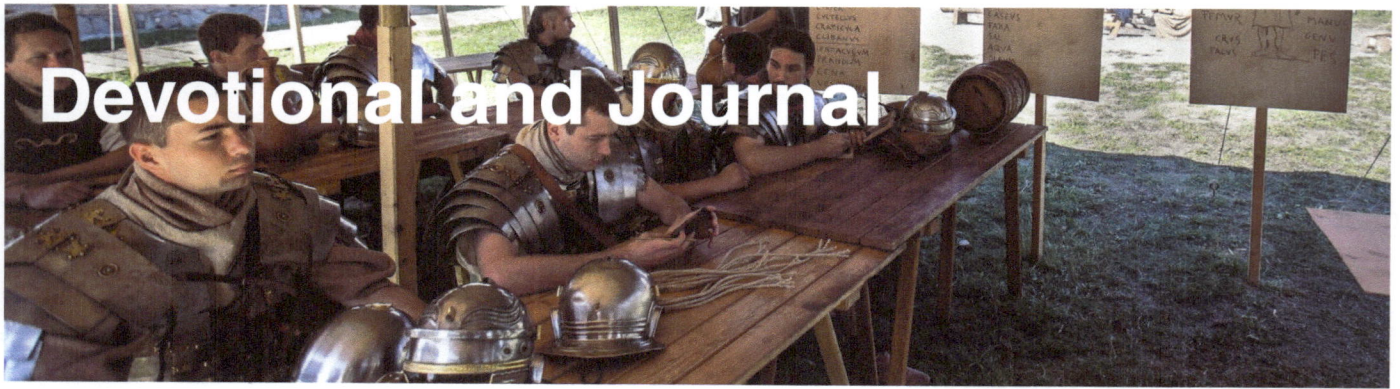

Devotional and Journal

Dear Gentlemen,

Your enemy is not flesh and blood, but your fight is against rulers; against the authorities; against the powers of this dark world and against the spiritual forces of evil in the heavenly realms.

(Ephesians 6:12)

In order to defeat your enemy, you must <u>Know your enemy's objectives:</u>

#1 he hates God, so:

#2 he hates what God loves;

#3 he knows he can't win, so he takes on the spoiler role;

#4 he seeks to kill and destroy people before they know Christ;

#5 he desires to discredit Christians because he hates God;

#6 he loves to kill people to hurt God,

and he loves to hurt Christians... because that hurts God.

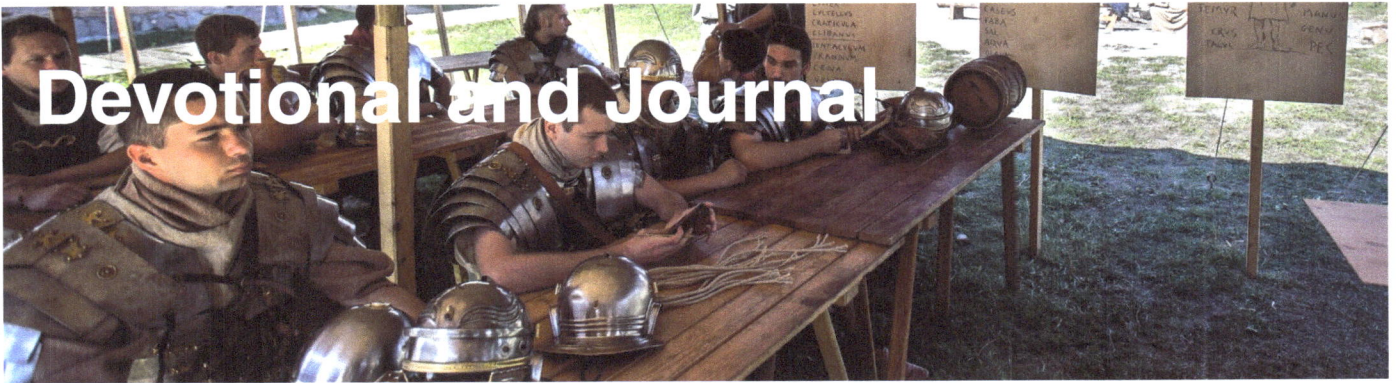

Devotional and Journal

Dear Gentlemen,

In this 10th week of discipleship, I ask you to look at a most provocative job description.

In 1st Peter 2:9, the Scripture says:

"But you are a chosen people, a royal priesthood, a holy nation, God's special possession, that you may declare the praises of Him who called you out of darkness into His wonderful light."

(read & chew)

Herein lies your purpose in life as a fighting unit: that you may DECLARE the praises of Him who saved you. I have a question for you to ponder...Did Jesus save you so that you could just get your personal salvation fix?...Or did He, on the other hand, by His design and purpose, have us participate as the mouthpieces or megaphones of the gospel? The word that is used here for "declare" in the Greek is "eks-än-ge'l-lō;" It is from where we get our word "exegete." Paul is telling us to "tell out" from or "tell fourth" in the declarative fashion as the Kerusso (the town crier), the Good News of Christ! In essence, we are taught to yell to the world.

"Hear ye, hear ye, I'm telling all the world that Jesus Christ saved me from my simple, depressing life, and He has promised me eternal life, so I praise Him above all names! And this same salvation that I have received, you can receive as well!"

"The conversion of a soul is the miracle of a moment,
the manufacture of a saint is the task of a lifetime...
With that wisdom in mind, be patient with others (and with yourself).
Maturity takes time."

- Alain Redpath

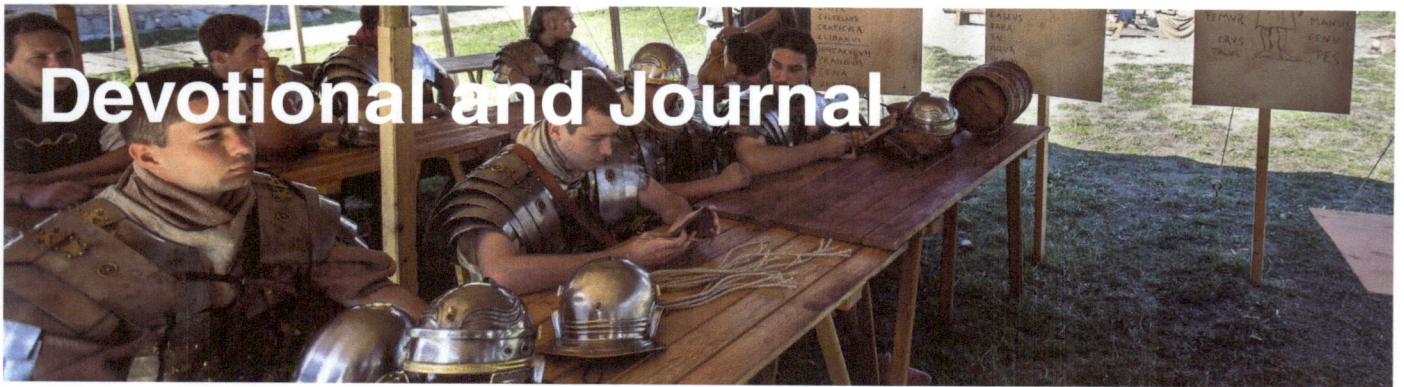

Devotional and Journal

Dear Gentlemen,

You are standing in one of the greatest points in history. You're going to have the opportunity to step into one of the greatest times of harvest and revival the world has ever known. I invite you to be preachers of the Gospel, and be known as Heralds.

Let's look at Romans 10:13 (read & chew)

and following:

"For whoever shall call upon the name of the Lord shall be saved."

Paul then asked:

"How can they call on Him they have not believed?"

(they don't know about Him yet)

Paul goes on to say,

"and how will they believe in Him of whom they have not heard?"

He then finishes by saying,

"and how shall they hear without a preacher?"

(the Greek word here is "Kerusontos;" translated: a herald or preacher)

That's where your life meets up with God's plan for this world!

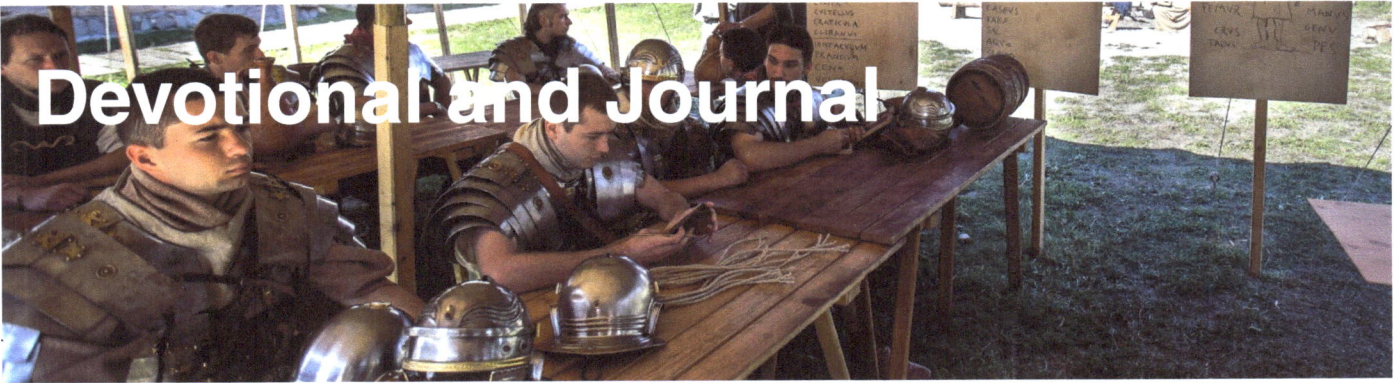

Devotional and Journal

Dear Gentlemen,

Yesterday, we looked at our purpose; today, we will explore the map and the directions we were given as to where to preach.

Mark 16:15 says,

"and He said to them, 'you go therefore, into all the world and preach (Kerusso) the gospel to every creature.'"

(read & chew)

This is why we are committed to missions around the world. We are partnering with millions of Christians around the world to get the Good News delivered to a lost and dying world. With modern technologies and transportation encircling the globe, any point can be reached in a maximum of 22 hours. We can reach the world, if we so desire, but we must be intentional about going and setting our hearts to do this.

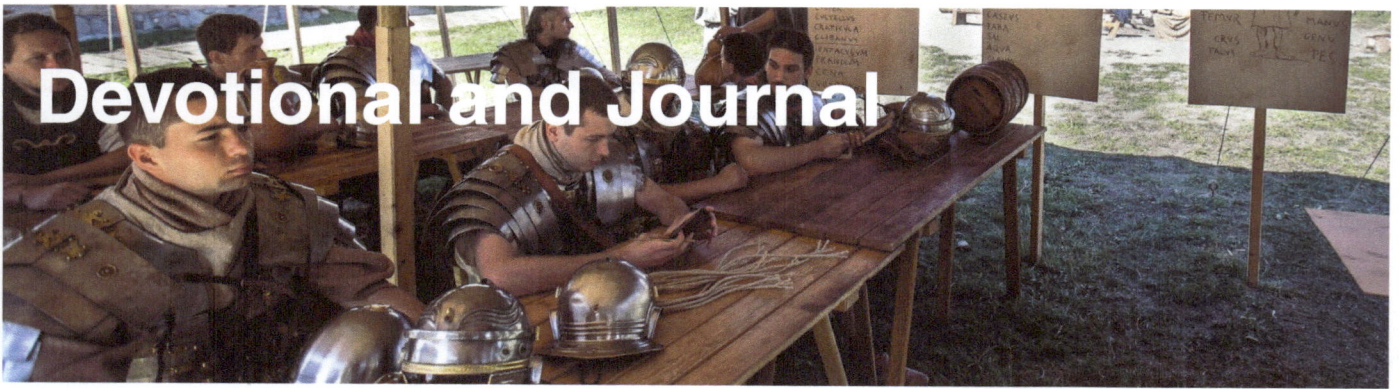

Devotional and Journal

Dear Gentlemen,

The most dangerous time in the Christian's life is between the time of his baptism and the time he leads his first person to Christ. The majority of the people in the American church at-large have never led anyone to Christ, much less made a disciple of them. This brings up huge questions as to what in the world they are doing with their time if they are not winning people to Christ? The Great Commission is the Christian's prime directive; and it is our mission goal as a church unit.

It is In the period between salvation and baptism, and leading their first-person to Christ, that most attenders go into a deep sleep that resembles a spiritual coma. There, they slip into a self-centered lifestyle that gets a "religious fix," as long as it's not too convicting. Not only is this not acceptable, but part of what we are teaching you to do is to be a herald to the church calling the church back to her first love.

Revelation 2:4

"Nevertheless, I have this against you, that you have left your first love. Remember therefore from where you have fallen; repent and do the first works, or else I will come to you quickly and remove your lamp stand from its place—
unless you repent.

(read & chew)

Your commitment to this path will show others that they can call out the Good News too!

"There's some task which the God of all the universe, the great Creator, your redeemer in Jesus Christ has for you to do, and which will remain undone and incomplete until by faith and obedience you step into the will of God."

- Alan Redpath

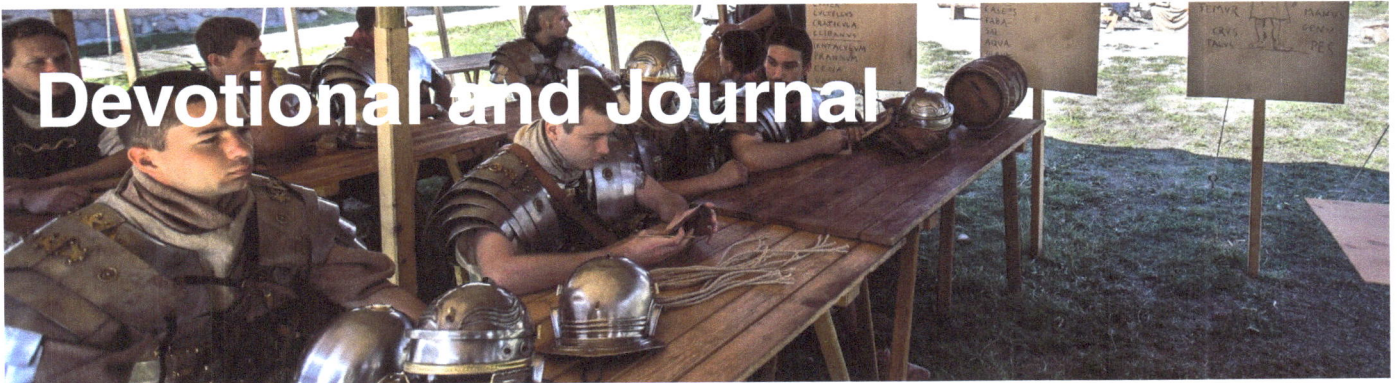

Devotional and Journal

Dear Gentlemen,

Now, here's a warning about proclaiming the gospel. You were designed to fight as a unit. This "calling out" is more effective the more we coordinate our attack.

Paul said this, in Ephesus 3:10 – 12,

"His intent was that now, through the church, the manifold wisdom of God should be made known to the rulers and authorities in heavenly realms, according to His eternal purpose that He accomplished in Christ Jesus our Lord!"

(read & chew)

This means God's purpose is for us to impact not just the earth, but the heavenly realms. I'll bet you never comprehended the scope of the impact of your preaching. Preaching is one of the most awesome opportunities in God's kingdom, and He did not choose angels to preach and us to support them. He chose us to preach and the angels to support us!

"There is nothing—no circumstance, no trouble, no testing—that can ever touch me until, first of all it has gone past God and past Christ, right through to me. If it has come that far, it has come with a great purpose, which I may not understand at the moment. But as I refuse to become panicky – as I lift up my eyes to Him – and as I accept it as coming from the throne of God for some great purpose of blessing to my heart, no sorrow will ever disturb me, no trial will ever disarm me, no circumstance will cause me to fret – for I shall rest in the joy of what my Lord is. That is the rest of victory."

- Alan Redpath

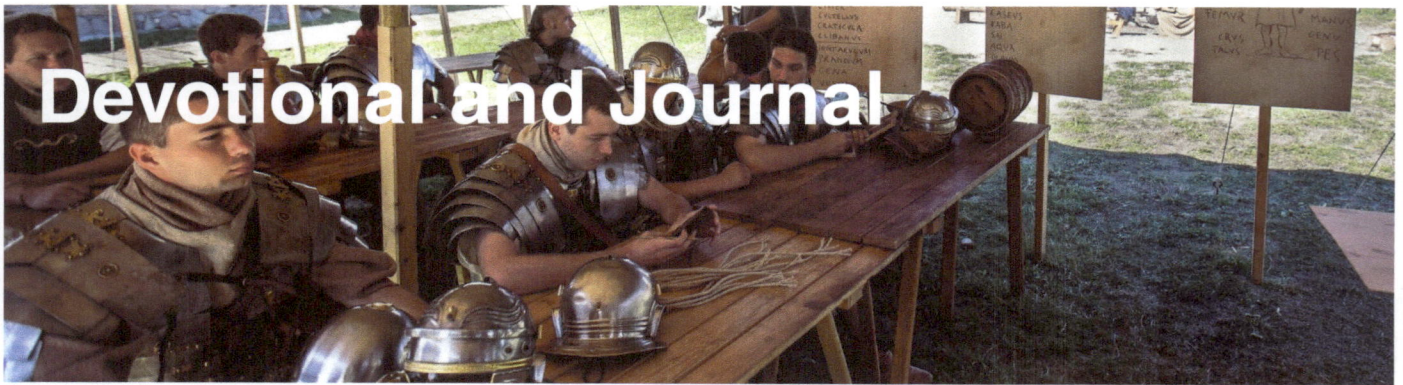

Dear Gentlemen,

As you are preaching, know this:

"whatever happens, conduct yourselves in a manner worthy of the gospel of Christ."
Philippians 1:27

(read & chew)

Remember, men, you are on duty 24/7. As for your mission and conduct: you are always being watched, both by the skeptical, who are looking for an excuse not to believe in your God based on your behavior, and by the hopeful, who are looking to your example for encouragement and to increase in their faith!

Paul then said this, and I love it: "then whether I come and see you or only hear about you in my absence, I will know that you stand firm in one spirit, striving together as one for the faith in the gospel without being frightened in any way by those who oppose you."

We fight as an interlocked unit. We leave no man behind!

"It takes more than a busy church, a friendly church, or even an evangelical church to impact a community for Christ. It must be a church ablaze, led by leaders who are ablaze for God."

- Wesley L. Duewel

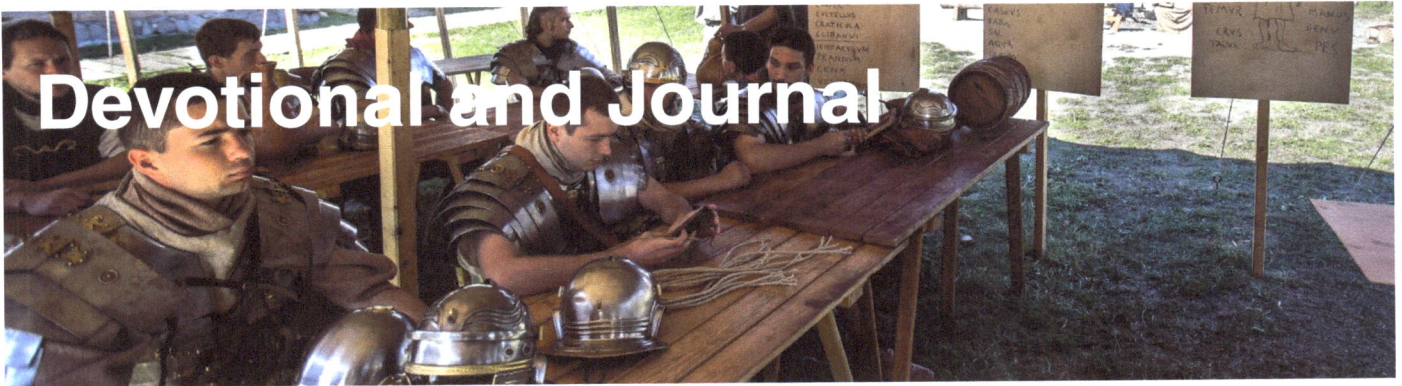

Devotional and Journal

Dear Gentlemen,

I have saved Jesus' last words in final instructions for this last day of your daily readings. Last words always carry a heavy weight. They were planned and perfectly spoken with God clarity, from the heart of Jesus and the Father, to us.

(read & chew Matthew 28:16)

"Then Jesus came to them and said, all authority in heaven and earth has been given to me…" In essence, Jesus is saying: "based on My godhood and everything I am, I want you to take to heart My next words." "Therefore go (based on my authority, go) and make disciples… This is what you are, and what you will be doing for the rest of your life!… Make disciples of all nations."

The word Nations is the word *"Ethnos"* in the Greek, and it refers to people groups. Notice Jesus uses the word "make." Disciples don't just happen, they are made! Part of that process involves them being baptized by you, and by the discipling being done by you! That's why Jesus goes on to say:

"baptizing them in the name of the Father, the Son, and the Holy Spirit, and teaching them to obey everything I have commanded."

In 2nd Timothy 2:1–3 Paul says: "you then, my sons, be strong in the grace that is in Christ Jesus, and the things you have heard me say in the presence of many witnesses, entrust to reliable people who will be qualified to teach others." (read & chew) He also says, "what you have heard from me, pass on the faithful men." So my ending question for you is: will this stop with you, or will you pass it on?

A final quote from Alan Redpath:

"We need men so possessed by the Spirit of God that God can think his thoughts through our minds, that he can plan his will through our actions, that he can direct his strategy of the world evangelism through his church."

Bible Study

1. Preparation
a. Time & Place
b. Bible
c. Notebook
d. Prayer

2. Observation
a. List Hist. Facts
b. What does it say?

3 Interpretation
a. What does it mean?
b. List principles

4. Application
a. Meaning to me?
b. List of self app.
c. Personalize

5. Meditation
a. Listen
b. Write prayer out
c. Ask for share
   opportunity

www.ingramcontent.com/pod-product-compliance
Lightning Source LLC
Chambersburg PA
CBHW060810090426

42737CB00002B/26